House Groups

DECLARING THE FAITH

House Groups

MICHAEL SKINNER

*The Revd Michael Skinner,
Principal of Wesley House
Cambridge
~~——~~ Died in
Aug 2008*

EPWORTH PRESS & SPCK

© *Michael Skinner 1969*
First published in 1969 by
Epworth Press and SPCK
Printed in Great Britain by
Cox & Wyman Limited
London, Fakenham and Reading

SBN 7162 0126 7 (Epworth)
SBN 281 02343 X (SPCK)

Contents

Acknowledgements

The author is grateful to the following for permission to include in this book extracts from other works: Birmingham Council of Churches (*Responsibility and the Welfare State?*); Iona Community (George MacLeod, *Only One Way Left*); Lutterworth Press (Hendrik Kraemer, *A Theology of the Laity*); Macmillan and Co. and Mrs W. Temple (William Temple, *Readings in St John's Gospel*); James Nisbet and Co. (Leonard Hodgson, *The Doctrine of Atonement*); S.C.M. Press (J. A. T. Robinson, *On Being the Church in the World*); World Council of Churches (Hans-Ruedi Weber, 'The Church in the House', *Laity*, April 1957). Quotations from the Bible are from the *Revised Standard Version*, copyright Thomas Nelson and Sons Ltd, 1946 and 1952, and from the *New English Bible*, copyright Oxford and Cambridge University Presses, 1961, by kind permission of the publishers.

Preface

FOR twenty-five years I have been an unashamed fanatic about house groups. This book makes no apology for such fanaticism but seeks to justify it on biblical grounds, as well as on the score of contemporary needs and practical politics.

It is designed not only for individual consumption, but for study by house groups or by groups of local church leaders contemplating the possibility of house groups. Questions are appended to each chapter for the purpose of group discussion as well as of individual meditation. It is suggested that Chapters 2 and 4 may be taken more conveniently in two parts, and if these divisions are adopted, the book will provide a group study for twelve sessions, and for thirteen if Appendix A on the traditional Methodist class meeting is treated as an additional chapter.

The book is written out of an experience of many different churches, all of which have taught me much, but I wish to record a very special debt to my friends at Old Elvet Church, Durham, who courageously embarked upon a full-blooded house group enterprise during my ministry there. Without them this book could not have been written. I take leave to dedicate to them what I have written, in gratitude for their showing to me and to many others how the local church can be renewed and become once again the exciting community it ought to be.

My thanks are also due to the Reverend A. W. Hopkins, Chaplain of the Leys School, Cambridge, who has kindly read my manuscript and made many valuable suggestions.

Wesley House, Cambridge
September 1969

1. Now is the Time for House Groups

THE cell or group movement has been important in the history of the Church from the days when Jesus called twelve that they might be with him and Paul could address greetings to 'the Church in the house'. In the last forty years, although the traditional Methodist class meeting has declined, there has been a revival of house groups – of groups meeting in members' homes – both under the auspices of the main Christian confessions and outside of them. This revival calls for a closer examination of the proper structure and purpose of house groups in contemporary society, for only if they are soundly based, efficiently organized, and clear-sighted as to their aims, will they fulfil their vital role.

Not everyone agrees that this is the time for house groups. Some object to them on the grounds that ordinary Christians are not yet ready for the exacting demands that groups make upon their members. Others argue that the need for house groups is a thing of the past, since the importance of the home locality is diminishing and with it that of the local church and its attendant house groups. The one school of thought considers house groups to be ahead of the times, the other behind the times. Let us examine these points of view in turn.

Is the Church not yet ready for house groups? They do indeed make heavy demands upon the average person who goes to

1

church to be ministered unto rather than to minister. Such a passive creature, it is argued, cannot be converted into an active one; such a person inarticulate in the realm of spiritual truths cannot be transformed into an articulate one. The ordinary church member is essentially a sheep and not a shepherd, someone to be saved rather than an ambassador for the Saviour.

There is no point in quarrelling with the opinion that the average churchgoer is 'sheepish', though we should add that this may not be so much his fault as that of his minister and of the Church tradition into which both have entered. Cardinal Gasquet illustrated the 'sheepish' state of the layman in his story of a priest's answer to an inquiry about the role of the layman in the Roman Catholic Church. (The answer, given many years ago, would have been equally applicable to the role of the layman in a great many Protestant Churches.) 'The layman,' said the priest, 'has two positions. He kneels before the altar; that is one. And he sits below the pulpit; that is the other.' Cardinal Gasquet thought it necessary to qualify this description of sheer passivity with the addendum that the layman also puts his hand in his pocket.

The fact that today the well-informed, both Roman and Protestant, recognize this conception of the Christian layman to be a travesty of the New Testament picture of him does not, unfortunately, necessarily mean that we know how passive sheep (I Peter 5:2) are to become also active ministers (I Peter 4:10) and active priests (I Peter 2:9). We recognize the objective, but are not confident that we have the means to achieve it. Even if we agree with Hendrik Kraemer that the laity are the Church's 'frozen credits', we may doubt whether they can be defrosted. The prescription of the kind of house groups described in this book is based on the assumption that the credits can be thawed out. But can they? Can the dumb spirit really be exorcized from the average layman? Can the local church really be turned inside out? Can it become the servant church of the neighbourhood? Is it prepared to lose itself in the service of Christ and the gospel, dying and rising with its Head? In such scepticism there is much force generated by experience.

Part of my answer to these questions may be given here. It is this – that unless we reach for the stars we shall never become airborne. Even though our reach exceed our grasp, the local church will at least be lifted out of the rut in which it often finds itself at present. Only by God-given vision and ambition shall we avoid perishing.

Now for the 'behind the times' school of thought. Here house groups are objected to as being part and parcel of the local church, that is, the church of a particular area of residence. In the opinion of not a few thinkers, the day of the local church is all but over, and with its demise must go the idea of house groups.

The question of house groups thus becomes a question of the local church. Has the local church really 'had it'? We may agree with much of the sociologists' diagnosis of the present situation without drawing the negative conclusion that the local church has had its day and will soon cease to be. The diagnosis can be summarized in the dictum that many people no longer 'live where they live'. That is to say, in this age of rapid urbanization people tend to sleep in one area, work in another, and play in yet a third, whereas in the medieval village and before the on-rush of urbanization they did all three in one locality. The result is that the local Church is no longer at the centre of everyday life as it was when a complete, self-contained community clustered around it. It is, for instance, absent from many realms where large portions of our lives are spent, and where the society of the future is being shaped. Because more and more government agencies, factories, businesses, communication industries, and places of advanced education are geographically separated from the areas where people have their homes and where local churches are found, the influence of the Church, it is argued, is not felt in these vital spheres.

Colin Williams, author of the much-read *Where in the World?*

3

and *What in the World?*,[1] puts the point in an article in the *Ecumenical Review* for January 1964. 'It is now true,' he writes, 'that in many of the places where basic decisions are made, energies expended and anxieties formed, the presence of Christ in word, sacrament and fellowship, is not provided.' In more positive vein, Bishop Lesslie Newbigin, in his sane little book *Honest Religion for Secular Man*,[2] can affirm that 'the Church must be where men are, speak the language they speak, inhabit the world they inhabit. This is the simplest of missionary principles.'

The conclusion that some draw from this is that we no longer need the local church with its house groups. They say we need factory groups, groups in Parliament and local government, among businessmen, economists, and television planners, a Church presence which will include preaching and sacraments as well as fellowship. It is significant, however, that the negative part of this conclusion – that the local church is obsolete – is not subscribed to either by Williams or Newbigin, or even by Harvey Cox in his brilliant best-seller, *The Secular City*. They sign no death-warrant for the local church. For them it is not a question of 'either–or' but of 'both–and'; a Church presence *both* in the realms of commerce and administration *and* in the areas of residence.

Let us by all means have the Church operational in all possible spheres. If this book is concerned mainly with house groups based on the local residential church, this is not to deny the needs of other kinds of groups. Moreover, house groups may be seen partly as an invaluable training-ground for these non-house groups. E. R. Wickham, in his seminal book *Church and People in an Industrial City*,[3] describes how the Methodist class meeting helped train men to play a very active part in so-called 'secular' spheres. Class meetings, he avers, 'produced an active and articulate laity – at least great numbers of them – such as

[1] Epworth Press.
[2] S.C.M. Press, p. 112.
[3] Lutterworth Press, p. 268–9.

4

no other denomination has produced, not only within the Connexion but in secular society, as the leadership given by great numbers of Methodists in the early Friendly Societies, Trades Union and Co-operative Societies shows.' If the class meeting could be the means of training men for such service, the house group can also prepare men and women for Christian witness in the world, whether in secular movements or in the new kinds of Christian presence we have mentioned. If the house group did nothing else than this – and, as we shall see, it can achieve far more – it could claim a valuable place in contemporary society.

If the reader feels that the case for the retention of the local church has been made, he can skip the next page or two and rejoin this chapter for the final two paragraphs. For the non-skippers here are three further arguments for the retention of the local church.

1. Community life in areas of residence has not altogether disappeared

In some areas a great many people, and not only women and children, still sleep, work, and play in the same neighbourhood. Granted that this may not be so true in twenty years' time as it is today, it nevertheless constitutes a warrant for the retention of the local church in such areas. Urbanization is not yet universal, nor does the motor-car take everybody away at the week-ends to caravan sites and country cottages.

2. Where there is no community life the Church must help to create it.

There is a glaring need for the Church to create a community, especially in those areas overtaken by urbanization. Here loneliness and the absence of any sense of belonging is a rampant social disease. The British Council of Churches, in its report *The Shape of the Ministry*, sees the mission of the local church to be

5

a vital one. 'Since the Church is, amongst other things, the place of *koinonia* (fellowship), one of its tasks must be to create conditions in which community can be found. This will mean, almost certainly, the breaking down of the large congregation (assuming that it exists) into smaller groups where relationships may be more truly personal: it will also mean the development of groups where those not of the congregation may find some form of community life. It will do this both as part of its service to the community and as part of its evangelistic outreach.'

Of course there are many people in the modern secular city who are not lonely, as Harvey Cox points out; people who have friends and acquaintances all over the place and who do not want to add to the number those who happen to inhabit adjacent houses or flats. But there are many others who are not so rich in friends, or not so mobile; people with no one to turn to in case of trouble, people longing for acceptance and friendship from their neighbourhood. These (and others), not least those on new housing estates, constitute a field white unto harvest for the missionary-minded local church.

3. *The importance of home makes the area of residence important*

The local church can still be a meaningful institution for those who value home life, even in areas where most other vestiges of natural community life have long since disappeared. The residential district is not to be written off as a mere 'dormitory', even though most of the men and many of the women commute to the city five days a week. Though Horst Symanowski and others may be right in affirming that industrial workers are influenced more by their hours at work than by their time at home, it is still true that for them home can be one of the vital influences of their lives, even when shift-work tends to disrupt the rhythm of family life.

Home is certainly the most important sphere for most mothers and their children. Admittedly women are less at home than they used to be, and this trend will increase when, with earlier

6

marriages, children are off their hands by the time early middle age has arrived. But even then home will remain at least the base of operations for most of them. This being so, the church which is situated in the homes of the people will continue to be at the centre of a very meaningful part of human existence. It will not be, or need not be, a ship left high and dry by an outgoing tide destined never to return. What is more, if the local church can learn to express itself in house groups as well as in Sunday services, it will indeed be marrying religion to home life, which for many people is a very dear, if not the most valued part of existence.

One further point can be added under this third heading. If the object of planting the church in industrial and political circles is not only to 'Christianize the structures' of these important realms, but also to bring people to Christ, will not the worker or politician so converted rightly expect to find some Christian organization in his home area to which he can seek to attach the members of his family who do not commute to the city? May he not want to find and to serve Christ in his home neighbourhood as well as in the sphere of work – especially as, with the increase in leisure hours (for industrial workers if not for politicians) he may find himself spending a higher proportion of his waking hours at home? Surely such a convert would value house groups not only for his own edification but as a means of Christian service and witness.

No further defence, it seems to me, is needed against those who would denigrate the local church and its house groups as things of the past. Indeed, it would appear that they are very much things of the present and future. There is a marked increase in house groups in most denominations in this and other countries. Methodists are learning to re-clothe their old class meeting in modern dress. Anglicans were inspired by Canon Southcott's imaginative experiment in Halton, Leeds. All Christians were exhorted by the World Council of Churches' Assembly at Evanston to take the Church into the house. House groups, in one form or another, have become fashionable.

7

Therein lies a danger, for it is possible to initiate groups without being at all clear as to their precise purpose, and with insufficient preparation. The house is too often built on sand, and nemesis descends after a year or two. Two of the aims of this book, therefore, are to suggest a rationale for house groups and to indicate the kind of preparation that may be necessary before embarking upon them so that, by careful thought and planning, this disaster may be avoided.

Questions for meditation and discussion

In this chapter we have been considering two objections to house groups – they are ahead of the times; they are behind the times. We will have one question on each objection.

Those who object that the Church is not ready for house groups stress the fact that the average layman is in spiritual matters more like a sheep than a shepherd. Question 1 is therefore this:

IS THE LAYMAN CAPABLE OF DOING MORE THAN DESCRIBED IN CARDINAL GASQUET'S STORY? CAN HE BE HELPED TO BECOME ARTICULATE ABOUT HIS FAITH?

Those who object to house groups as being out of date stress their conviction that the local church has ceased to have a role in modern society. Question 2 is therefore this:

CAN YOU SEE THE LOCAL CHURCH AS RELEVANT IN AN URBAN SOCIETY?

2. It is Always the Time for Christian Fellowship

PERSEVERE with this chapter, read it at least twice if necessary, for it is quite vital for the right understanding of the nature of the house groups discussed in this book. It will also provide useful background material for the study outline to be found in Appendix B at the end of this book. As this is a long chapter you may like to divide it into two. I have indicated a suitable half-way house.

Most Englishmen consider that it is possible to be a Christian without being involved in fellowship with other Christians. You can be a Christian, they say, without going to church. I met one such Englishman in a train some years ago. He insisted on talking to me when I wanted to get on with some work. I had rejoiced when the compartment emptied at the previous station, spread my pages of notes on the Epistle to the Ephesians down one side of the compartment and started to work. My joy was short-lived. As the train was clearing the platform, the carriage door was violently wrenched open and a young man scrambled into the seat diagonally opposite to me, panting for breath. Before he had recovered half his breath, and without the slightest encouragement from the would-be worker who was not intent on practising fellowship that morning, he started to tell me all about himself.

He was a builder in a town farther up the line. He boasted that his firm put up houses twice as fast as any other firm in the area. I tried to stem the torrent of eloquence with the curt remark that this was nothing to boast about since houses were going up desperately slowly at that time. Quite undismayed, he went on talking, and so I decided to ask him what a cornerstone was in a modern building. (Christ, you will remember, is referred to as a cornerstone in Ephesians 2:20 as well as in 1 Peter 2:6.) He explained to me in considerable detail how indeed it was the crucial stone, how it had to be set at exactly the right angle, else the whole building would be askew, how it had to be set by a skilled craftsman, and so on. I suppose we talked for some twenty minutes about the erection of modern houses.

After a time he turned to me and my lay attire, glanced at the papers scattered along the seat, and remarked in a tone of only slightly-disguised contempt, 'I suppose you are a schoolmaster.' I replied that though I was wearing an ordinary collar and tie I was nevertheless a parson. His jaw dropped fast and far and, what was worse, the gap between the upper and lower lip showed no signs of closing. Fearing the onset of lockjaw and not knowing what to do, I hazarded the remark that I was a Methodist parson. This chance remark, born of desperation rather than denominational pride, worked wonders. A look of indescribable relief flooded over his face, the gap was at least halved, and after an interval of unusual quiet he was able to inform me that he had once attended a Methodist Sunday School. I asked him whether he still went to church and he replied that he went occasionally to the Harvest Festival and to the Sunday School Anniversary. Seeing I was disappointed that he did not go to church more often, he hastened to assure me that nevertheless he was a Christian. He proceeded to give me a list of the vices that he shunned, and another list of the virtues he espoused, the latter coming to an impressive climax with the solemn information that he was always very honest with his wife.

It seems to me that this very pleasant young man is typical of so many of our fellow-countrymen. He tried to follow the ethical teaching of Christ, in so far as he knew and understood it, but he did not believe in the Church. Gallup Polls on the state of religion in this land seem to suggest that only 15 per cent of the people in this country profess to believe in the Church, though 65 per cent profess to believe in Christ as divine. Despite John Wesley's dictum, it is popularly believed that you can be a solitary Christian.

The New Testament has two very clear words to say to that young man and to so many like him. It is good that prospective members of house groups should understand these two words because a good house group is going to find itself in dialogue with people like that young man. The two words are *faith* and *fellowship*.

The builder needed to be told about *faith*, for Christian faith means trust in Christ and the end of trust in ourselves. It means that we do not talk about Christianity exclusively or primarily in terms of what *we* do, as this young man did with his lists of vices avoided and virtues practised. Rather we talk of Christianity as trust in what *God in Christ* has done for us. 'The life I now live in the flesh,' declared St Paul, 'I live by faith in the Son of God, who loved me and gave Himself for me.'

The mature Christian, then, is first and foremost someone who can sing:

> Nothing in my hands I bring,
> Simply to Thy cross I cling;
> Naked, come to Thee for dress;
> Helpless, look to Thee for grace;
> Foul, I to the fountain fly;
> Wash me, Saviour, or I die.

This hymn shows how the converted man has turned away from self-trust to trust in Christ, how he has become as a little child. A little child trusts instinctively in his parents' goodness; he does not try to earn it, or deserve it, or pay for it. Such goodness is not for sale. It is essentially a gift. It is not for employees or Pharisees trusting in what they have done, but for infants and

11

tax-gatherers who know where to turn for mercy and love. Read Luke 18:9–14.

The second thing to notice about faith is that it is the gift of the Holy Spirit. Jesus evokes this trust in Himself only when the Holy Spirit has given us eyes to see Him. Without the aid of the Holy Spirit we cannot acclaim Jesus as Lord, cannot perceive His Divinity. See I Corinthians 12:3 and the great hymn of Charles Wesley that draws inspiration from that verse:

> Spirit of faith, come down,
> Reveal the things of God . . .
>
> No man can truly say
> That Jesus is the Lord,
> Unless Thou take the veil away,
> And breathe the living word;
> Then, only then, we feel
> Our interest in His blood,
> And cry, with joy unspeakable:
> Thou art my Lord, my God!

Faith, then, is Spirit-given trust in Jesus and Him crucified. The third thing to say about it is that it is accompanied by love. When the Holy Spirit shows us Jesus, shows us what our brains cannot discover nor our physical eyes perceive, shows us what the disciples needed Pentecost to apprehend, He evokes in us not only faith in Jesus but love for Him, love for all He has done for us, love for all that He was and is. True faith and love are inseparable. The one implies the other. When we are given this faith-love we are united to Christ the crucified and risen Lord. And being so united to Christ what shall be our relationship to others so united?

Now we are ready for the second word to the builder, *fellowship*. Fellowship is one of the fruits of faith and love, and so is a product of the Holy Spirit, the Giver of faith and love. In this way we can refer to the Church as the fellowship of the Holy Spirit. We will discuss this fellowship of the Holy Spirit first in terms of the breaking down of the middle walls of partition (if you have a Bible beside you, keep it open at Ephesians 2) and secondly in terms of mutual ministry. We will call the first extensive fellowship and the second intensive fellowship.

First, then, *extensive fellowship*. St Paul explains this in the second chapter of Ephesians, verses 11–22. This famous passage follows the equally famous description of saving faith in verses 8–10. The fellowship in Christ expounded in the later passage follows quite naturally from that faith in God's grace defined in the earlier one. 'The fact is this,' St Paul can be represented as saying. 'If you have the Spirit-given faith in Christ and Him crucified, and you meet someone who shares with you this tremendous gift of God, you should realize that you are bound to him by the greatest bond this universe can provide. The other man may be a Gentile and you a Jew, but though your races have been at daggers drawn for centuries, though there has been this appalling, impenetrable middle wall of partition between your race and his, once you have been put in the way of receiving Christ and His dying love, that wall is no more. What you have now in common is stronger than what kept you apart.' So we might paraphrase St Paul's teaching that Christ 'is our peace, who has made both one, and has broken down the middle wall of hostility'.

I remember a famous headmaster of a Methodist Public School telling an undergraduate congregation of a moving experience he had while attending an educational conference in France. He had found himself sharing a bedroom with a Roman Catholic teacher, and as they were both undressing on the first night, the Methodist began to wonder what the Roman would think of him if he were to adopt his ordinary practice for his evening devotions, kneeling down to read his Bible and to pray. The Roman was a perceptive Christian, realized what was going on in the mind of the headmaster, and said very simply, 'I love Jesus; do you?' The Methodist also affirmed his love for his Lord and the knowledge of His love for him, and their ecclesiastical divisions seemed to melt away

13

into nothingness as both men pursued their evening devotions. A common faith and love meant fellowship.

Christians today are increasingly realizing that in having Christ and His salvation they possess the greatest bond in the universe. This realization prompts them to seek a more adequate expression of the great unity Christ has already given to believers. Reunion schemes, it seems to me, have somehow to reflect this given unity in Christ, without attempting to supplement it as though Christ's work, sufficient to unite believers to God, proves insufficient to unite them to one another.

The middle walls of partition have, of course, to go down not only between denominations, but within local churches as well. Here not only race barriers, but social barriers and sex barriers have to be demolished. According to St Paul, for believers 'there is neither Jew nor Greek, there is neither slave nor free, there is neither male nor female; for you are all one in Christ Jesus' (Galatians 3:28).

To sum up what we have been saying about fellowship in its *extensive* aspect: The Spirit-given faith in Christ, accompanied as it is by love, overcomes all divisions for those who possess it. As I tried to explain to the builder in the train, Christianity is essentially a religion of fellowship. I pointed out to him that he had been showing me the way to put up houses, joining one brick to another, and that this was precisely how St Peter describes Christianity – in terms of living stones built up into a spiritual house of which Jesus is the cornerstone. Coming in faith to Jesus, the cornerstone, means coming to those who are already joined to Him. We cannot have Jesus by Himself. Read I Peter 2:4–7.

If you are using this book in a weekly group, this is probably the place to stop, leaving the rest of the chapter for next time. Group discussion on the chapter so far might centre round two questions:

1. WHAT WOULD HAVE BEEN YOUR ANSWER TO THE BUILDER IN THE TRAIN?

14

2. IF BY SPIRIT-GIVEN FAITH WE ARE UNITED TO CHRIST, OUGHT
   NOT CHRISTIANS OF DIFFERENT DENOMINATIONS BE ABLE TO
   GATHER TOGETHER AT THE LORD'S TABLE?

For this second question you might like to consider St Paul's teaching in I Corinthians 10:16–17. His meaning would seem to be that when Christians partake of the Communion Bread in true faith they become automatically the Body of Christ, with all that means in terms of fellowship (see I Corinthians 12). Faith and fellowship once more go together.

Now for the *intensive* aspect of fellowship. Fellowship signifies more than the breaking down of middle walls of partition in respect of race, class, and sex, a breaking down of division which we have referred to as extensive fellowship. It means more than the adjacency left by the removal of barriers. It indicates also 'interaction' (to use a term much-beloved by the apostles of the modern science of group dynamics), the interaction described by St Paul in his famous picture of the Church as Christ's body, whose members practise mutual ministry. Read I Corinthians 12, especially verses 12–27. You can sit side by side with people in Church whom you do not know from Adam, and no doubt you are bound up with such people in the fellowship of worship. You are practising fellowship with them in its extensive, but not in its intensive aspect. You are ministering with them, but hardly to them. You know so little about them that you cannot enter into their sufferings and joys. With intensive fellowship, 'If one member suffers, all suffer together; if one member is honoured, all rejoice together' (I Corinthians 12:26). You cannot honestly say that you could not get on without them, for you do not stand with them in a relationship of interdependence. Yet with intensive fellowship, 'The eye cannot say to the hand, "I have no need of you," nor again the head to the feet, "I have no need of you." (I Corinthians 12:21.)

There can be no doubt that St Paul understands the Church as the body of Christ in terms of intensive as well as extensive fellowship. In this body every part has to be functioning

15

properly. Every Christian, that is, is to be an active minister. Ephesians 4:15–16 states that 'we are to grow up in every way into Him who is the head, into Christ, from whom the whole body, joined and knit together by every joint with which it is supplied, when each part is working properly, makes bodily growth and upbuilds itself in love'. Let me repeat, the phrase 'when each part is working properly' indicates that all members of the body of Christ are to be ministering members.

This is only one of four references to the ministry of all believers, sometimes called 'the total ministry of the Church', in Ephesians 4:1–16. Take another look at this tremendous passage with its revolutionary teaching. Every Christian has a call to ministry, according to verse 1. Every Christian is given grace for this ministry, according to verse 7. Every Christian is to be equipped by special ministers for the work of ministry, according to verses 11 and 12.

Much modern teaching about the ministry of the laity rightly insists that the Christian layman should be active in the world; but it perhaps does not always do full justice to the clear teaching of St Paul that the layman is bound to take part in this mutual ministry, giving and receiving ministry from his fellow-believers in his local church and neighbourhood. The New Testament regards such mutual ministry as essential to the life of the Church and the practice of the Christian religion. If you would study this aspect of the matter further, an aspect so obviously important for an understanding of the function of house groups, see I Corinthians 12:7 and 11, Romans 12:3–5, I Thessalonians 5:11, Hebrews 10:24–25 and, not least important, I Peter 4:10–11.

Many twentieth-century Christians would rather stop with the public transport kind of togetherness, mere propinquity to virtual strangers, than go along with the fireside kind where a group of friends help each other with their problems. One way of attempting to evade this challenge to a full-scale 'Body Christianity' (that is, to mutual ministry) would be to maintain that such fellowship was incidental to first-century Christianity, certainly not a rigid prescription for every age. Four arguments might be used to defend such a position:

1. The early Christians were being persecuted, and a persecuted minority always tends to huddle together.

In reply, we may agree that persecution helps to foster the fellowship of the Church, but emphatically deny that this was the *only* cause of fellowship in the primitive Church.

2. The early Christians practised fellowship because they were expecting an imminent end to the world. It is in the context of 'the end of all things is at hand' that I Peter 4:7–11 advocates Christian fellowship.

But it is in the same context, we might reply, that he also advocates keeping 'sane and sober for your prayers'. St Peter surely did not mean the early Christians to pray *only* because the end was thought to be at hand. His teaching is surely in accord with Hebrews 10:24–25 which makes the expectation of an early end to history merely an additional reason for fellowship: 'Let us consider how to stir up one another to love and good works, not neglecting to meet together, as is the habit of some, but encouraging one another, and *all the more* as you see the Day drawing near.'

3. First-century Christianity was characterized by the kind of religious excitement that generally accompanies periods of re-vival. People spoke in tongues, and the difficulty at Corinth (see I Corinthians 14) was not to open the mouths of a passive laity, but to tame the tongues of an excessively loquacious assembly and bring some order out of chaos. In such periods of religious excitement the Holy Spirit seems prodigal with His gifts of ministry, but not so prodigal in normal periods when the fires of revival have died down. You cannot honestly expect, we shall be told, the rank and file church members today to open their mouths and minister to one another in groups. Groups can only flourish in periods like the New Testament one.

Against this plea I would contend that necessity is as effective a stimulus to mutual ministry as religious excitement is. What I mean is this. If a person possesses any love for our Lord, any faith in Him for salvation, any knowledge of His love for us, then miracles may be expected to happen when that Christian finds a group or an individual in need of help or guidance. Faced by such necessity, and inspired by love for our Lord, the Christian will discover an accession of his natural powers. He will awake to the surprising fact that he has been given grace to minister to others. As John Donne, the Christian poet, put it, 'Grace finds out man's naturall faculties and exalts them to a capacity.' I have seen divine grace do just that with many people through and in house groups. No religious excitement is needed. Just loyalty to Jesus and the challenge of necessity.

Hendrik Kraemer gives a telling example of how necessity can produce lay ministry and bring I Corinthians 12 to life again. In *A Theology of the Laity*[1] he describes the plight of the German Evangelical Church in Silesia when it lost nearly all its pastors in the last war. Faced with the necessity of keeping their churches open, the lay people rose to the occasion and decided to share out the pastor's ministerial functions among themselves. The 'frozen credits' were defrosted.

4. It is an undisputed fact that the early Church met in private houses for some two hundred years, because the State forbade it to own [church property. (Occasionally Christians met in gravel pits, in the open air, in catacombs, but generally in one another's houses. See, for instance, Romans 16:3–22, I Corinthians 16:9, Colossians 4:15, Philemon 2, Acts 2:46 and 12:12.) For Jewish Christians the church meeting would be in 'a large upper room furnished and ready' (Mark 14:15). Palestinian houses would have the family rooms downstairs while the upper room, approached by outside steps, would run the whole length and breadth of the house. For Gentile Christians the meeting would be in a largish hall around which clustered the living-rooms. In heathen families there would be an altar in the hall

[1] Lutterworth Press.

18

and offerings to the family ancestors and their gods. In Christian families there would be a table replacing the heathen altar and emblems, a table on which the Eucharist would be celebrated. In the case of both the Jewish and Gentile houses the size of the congregation was bound to be limited. Everybody would know everyone else, and there would be mutual weeping and rejoicing.

The fourth argument, then, is that the New Testament is merely making a virtue out of a necessity. Since the early Christians were not allowed to have 'churches' but had to meet in groups of a limited size, it was inevitable that their fellowship should be an intimate one. But now that we have in many places large edifices, sometimes used by large congregations, such intimate fellowship, it could be argued, is no longer a practical proposition. 'Circumstances alter cases', and just as we no longer observe the New Testament practices of holy kissing and the covering of women's heads in worship, so we need no longer practise mutual ministry.

This plausible line of argument invites the following comments, which will in their turn help to summarize some of the conclusions of this chapter:

(a) Is the teaching about the Church as the body of Christ not relevant to the twentieth century?

I have never heard any informed Christian suggest that the description is out of date. Yet St Paul's main expositions of the concept of the ecclesial body of Christ are very much centred on mutual ministry. See I Corinthians 12, Romans 12, and Ephesians 4. What is more, his teaching about the ecclesial body (the Church) is closely linked with his teaching about the eucharistic body and the whole saving work of Christ in a way that holy kissing and other first century practices simply are not. The conclusion would seem to be that the ecclesial body, with its mutual ministry, is as permanent a part of Christianity as is the sacrament of Holy Communion. See once again, if you will, I Corinthians 10:16–17.

(b) Can we be satisfied with anything less than the fullest

19

possible expression of the unity that Christ has given to all who have faith in Him and His saving work?

We all agree that having Christ in common means that we Christians must love one another so much that denominational walls of partition collapse. Should we not equally agree that Christian love must have its maximum exercise *within* the local congregation as well as *between* the local congregations?

Sharing in Christ and His salvation must mean more than attendance at public worship with a crowd of people who continue to remain strangers to us. It must mean more than indulging in social gatherings on Church premises, though such gatherings may well have a place. It must mean more than belonging to a sectional group, addressed by outside speakers to whom the members passively listen. It must mean more than working side by side for bazaars and other church 'efforts', even if these are still necessary in an age of Christian stewardship. It must surely mean sharing the riches we have in Christ with one another; seeking to give and to receive as together we attempt to thrash out the problems of Christian belief and practice; seeking to express in a variety of ways our love for fellow-believers, to practise the fullest possible 'interaction' with them within a structure of interdependence. We should be aiming at nothing less than this, and since such intimate fellowship cannot be adequately practised by a large congregation, the need for subdivisions during the week becomes obvious. The formal dinner of public worship must be supplemented by the meal around the fireside of house groups.

(*c*) Do we not possess in house groups a wonderful additional way of preaching the gospel?

If mutual ministry, or intensive fellowship as we have termed it, represents the end product of Christ's saving work of reconciling men to God and to one another, then the advertising of it can be a proclaiming of Christ and His gospel. House groups composed on the basis of residence can show their neighbourhoods something of this end-product of the Saviour's work, not only in the weekly group meeting but outside it as well. (We

20

shall take up and amplify this point in Chapter 4.) Jesus Himself is reported to have said to His little group, 'By this all men will know that you are my disciples, if you have love for one another.' St Paul similarly connects mutual ministry with Christ. In making use of the analogy of the human body to describe the nature of the Church, he prefaces his treatment with the startling words, 'For just as the body is one and has many members, and all the members of the body, though many, are one body, so it is with *Christ*.' We might have expected the apostle to write, 'So it is with the *Church*.' Part of St Paul's meaning would seem to be that when Christians are found within this structure of body Christianity, there is Christ. The conclusion to be drawn is that in our making visible to the world such intimate fellowship and mutual love, Christ will be proclaimed, His gospel advertised.

We have arrived at a very different conception of Christianity from the one espoused by the builder in the train. He thought of the Christian religion in terms of a solo occupation like the card game, Patience. The New Testament teaching makes it clear that it is far more like soccer, essentially a team game where the players interact with one another and together fight to win. Christian fellowship, as we have seen, is bound up with Christian faith, faith which receives the Lord Jesus and all His benefits, faith which is a 'must' for every time and place. Fellowship is dependent on faith, not on persecution, the expected end to the world, religious revival or the absence of church buildings. It is rooted in Christian salvation, it is the natural reflection of the everlasting gospel and the anticipation of the rich community life of heaven. It is always the time for Christian fellowship.

Of course, if we are to have any chance of convincing the builder and those who think like him of this 'soccer' version of Christianity, we shall have not only to give our account of Christianity but, more important, show them the Church functioning as the body of Christ in their neighbourhood.

Meditation and discussion. In addition to the two questions given at the half-way stage of this chapter, the individual reader or the group may like to tackle the question:

DO YOU AGREE THAT THE CHRISTIAN IS BOUND TO PRACTISE MUTUAL MINISTRY?

An additional question, if required, could be:

DO YOU THINK THAT THE CHURCH GAINED AND LOST SOMETHING WHEN IT REMOVED ITS MEETINGS FROM PRIVATE HOUSES TO 'CHURCHES'?

3. It is Always the Time for Christian Mission

THE Church is meant to be an army as well as a family. It is certainly not meant to be a closed family circle, but an expanding one. It is not only a matter of

> Sweetly may we all agree,
> Touched with loving sympathy:
> Kindly for each other care;
> Every member feel its share.

It is also a matter of

> Onward! Christian soldiers,
> Marching as to war,
> With the Cross of Jesus
> Going on before.

> Christ, the royal Master,
> Leads against the foe;
> Forward into battle,
> See! His banners go.

One can put the images of the Church as a family and an army together and visualize the Church as essentially a missionary fellowship. It is vital that these two concepts are held together. As Lesslie Newbigin once put it, 'An unchurchly mission is as much a monstrosity as an unmissionary church.' By 'unchurchly

23

mission' he presumably meant to indicate that kind of mission hall where there was preaching for individual conversions, but where there was no fellowship to receive new converts. (I am not suggesting for a moment that all mission halls are in such a parlous condition.) The Church is meant to be far more than a preaching establishment for, as we have seen, it is composed of living stones built into a spiritual house, and its life is one of intensive as well as of extensive fellowship.

On the other hand – and this is as reprehensible as the 'un-churchly mission' – there are many local churches where there is a vigorous fellowship life of a kind, but where there is little or no sense of mission. Let us repeat, the local church must be a missionary fellowship or, if you will, a fellowship mission.

We find both fellowship and mission stressed in Mark 3:13–15, a passage in which we may discern the title deeds of the Church. As Jesus sets out to reconstitute the true Israel, He chooses twelve men 'to be sent out to preach and have authority to cast out demons'. In other words, a great part of the *raison d'être* of the Church is to be a missionary movement. As Hendrik Kraemer would say, 'the Church is mission'. Yes, but fellowship as well as mission, for Jesus chooses these twelve men 'to be with Him'. Being with Jesus, the cornerstone, meant being with the other living stones joined to Him. Those disciples could have Jesus in common only as they lived together in love, without quarrelling. They could not have Him for their own private possession, as they lived separated from each other by envy and selfish ambitions. To be with Jesus meant to be with the other eleven in a spirit of true Christian brotherhood. From the beginning the Church was marked out to be a missionary fellowship.

The next paragraph or two will continue this theme of the interconnection between mission and fellowship. Jesus called these disciples to be 'fishers of men'. To be a follower of Jesus meant indeed to be an apostle, that is, someone 'sent out' to preach the gospel. But Jesus saw these twelve men not just as individual witnesses to Him, but as a corporate witness. They

24

had worked together as a crew for their fish, and they would continue to do so for their human catch. By their team-work, by their mutual love, they would preach Christ. 'By this all men will know that you are my disciples, if you have love for one another.' If to be with Christ meant to be with one another in love, then to be with one another in love was a way of pointing men to the presence of Christ. Fellowship was one form of mission (see the last paragraph or two of the previous chapter). Together they were to form 'a city set on a hill', incapable of being hidden, fully visible to men. Together they were to be 'the light of the world', not hidden under bushels nor, we might add, always hidden away behind church doors. All this, of course, does not exclude the need for individual witness to the gospel, but it is not without significance that when the disciples were sent out to preach they went in pairs.

Other images and terms for the Church in the New Testament evoke this same picture of the Christian fellowship making an impact on the world. The Church is to act on its environment as salt on food. Our very word 'church' corresponds to the Greek word, *ekklesia* (from which comes our English adjective 'ecclesiastical'). *Ekklesia* could be literally rendered 'a calling out'. When it is used in the Greek version of the Old Testament it generally means, according to a famous scholar, 'the People of God assembled together for common action'. This is what it would also appear to mean in the New Testament, and should mean for us today. Such a meaning is reflected in St Peter's description of the nature of the Church to the Christians of Asia Minor: 'You are a chosen race, a royal priesthood, a holy nation, God's own people, that you may declare the wonderful deeds of Him who called you out of darkness into His marvellous light' (I Peter 2:9). What better description of the Church as a missionary fellowship could we have than this? Another is to be found in Weymouth's fine translation of Philippians 1:27: 'fighting shoulder to shoulder for the faith of the gospel.'

The Church, then, is a saving army. Its soldiers are being

saved; that is tremendously important. Even more important is the fact that they are part of a saving movement, described by such metaphors as light and salt. The Church, as has often been said, is not to be so much an ark for the saved, as an army for the Saviour to use. What a revolution would take place in many local churches if the emphasis were put on the army rather than on the ark. The Church would be turned inside out. But when Christians today talk, as they are increasingly doing, about the renewal of the church, about the local church's need for a missionary structure, nothing less than a revolution is contemplated.

It seems to me, however, that before it can be brought about, four lessons will have to be learnt by church members. Let us hope that they can be quickly learnt, for the time is short. A famous Presbyterian preacher once declared that it took him twenty-five years, preaching twice each Sunday, to change the ideas of his congregation on any great matter. Let us hope that five years would be sufficient for mastering the implications of regarding the Church more as an army than as an ark. We will spend the rest of the chapter explaining these four lessons.

Lesson 1: THE CHURCH DOES NOT EXIST FOR THE SAKE OF ITS BUILDINGS

Many faithful churchgoers have for years been so hard put to it to keep the fabric of their church buildings in reasonable repair that they would be quite lost if someone were to endow their Church with sufficient money to obviate for ever the necessity of bazaars and other 'efforts', or (more likely) if they were to have a successful Christian stewardship campaign resulting in trebled or quadrupled income. They have almost come to think that the main purpose of the Church of Christ is to keep church buildings in good condition; to fight not sin and unbelief so much as the death-watch beetle and woodworm; to improve not the spiritual temperature but to increase the degrees Fahrenheit in the cold church.

26

Yet no army, however effete, considers its main task to be keeping the barracks in repair. Nor does it go in for frequent bazaars and justify them on the grounds that they keep the troops together. An army does not exist to keep its buildings going, but to fight the enemy. Its barracks are extremely useful for much of the time, but the army is not absolutely dependent on them. It can live under canvas. If all church buildings were to be destroyed by fire the real Church in any locality could continue, for the real Church is living stones, a body all the members of which are priests commissioned to introduce God to men.

We do not in our better moments want to be deprived of our church premises. They are most useful bases, they provide a focal point for Christian community life, they have sacred associations for many; but they are not quite indispensable. As we have seen, the early Church flourished without them for the first two hundred years of its existence. We are certainly not required to bow down to bricks and mortar, nor to resist the closing of redundant or otherwise unnecessary edifices when the interests of a more effective mission call for fewer or better-sited premises.

Lesson 2: THE CHURCH DOES NOT EXIST PRIMARILY FOR THE SAKE OF ITS MEMBERS

An army does not exist primarily for the sake of its soldiers; they exist for the army and its cause. A good army will indeed look after its soldiers, if only because it cannot fight successfully unless it does so. But its supreme aim is to fight, or to be ready to fight a war as effectively as possible. Everything else is to subserve this main objective.

Many churchgoers have quite failed to transfer this emphasis on winning the war to the spiritual realm. They may sing, 'Like a mighty army moves the Church of God', but the excuses many of them make for cutting parades would look singularly silly in an army context: 'I don't go now, because I do not know the tunes the regimental bands play these days'; or 'I was not allowed to beat the big drum'; or 'Somebody in the platoon trod on my corns and insulted me'; or 'I can't stand the sergeant-major's voice and mannerisms'.

Such people are perhaps not very advanced in the spiritual life; but others, obviously much further on, also fail to see the Church as mission, with everyone in it 'fighting shoulder to shoulder for the faith of the gospel'. For them, the Church is a glorified spiritual soup-kitchen, to which they come at a certain hour on a Sunday. (The one visit generally proves sufficient nowadays, with the additional help provided by TV and radio spiritual fare.) The Church exists to give them sufficient nourishment to cope with their individual existences for the next six days. With perhaps such people in mind, a Monsignor is reported to have complained that for many the Church is no more than 'a sacramental filling-station'.

Let us, however, not be too hard, or appear to sneer at these people who tend to treat the Church as a means to their ends. Thank God that they still come for help, even though we might have hoped that after some years they would have been able to give the Church more of their time and talents. Perhaps, even so, we should blame not them but the church tradition into which both they and many ministers have entered and never tried very much to change. It is all a case, once again, of the good proving the enemy of the best.

This second lesson is going to be a very difficult one to learn. How hard it is to rid people of the idea that church services and meetings exist primarily for individual uplift! How hard it is to get across to them Symanowski's trenchant point that the real gulf is not between the pulpit and the pew, but between the congregation (including its minister) and the whole world of unbelievers. (Read Symanowski's stimulating book, *The Christian Witness in an Industrial Society*.)[1] We shall not find it easy to persuade house groups to be outward-looking, to expand, to bisect in the interests of mission, and not to relapse into cosy little cliques.

[1] Collins.

One reason why it is difficult for people to learn this second lesson is that the spiritual soup-kitchen concept of the Church has been in vogue for a thousand years and more, as we shall explain under Lesson 4. Not even the early Church found this business of mission easy. Acts 8:44ff would seem to suggest that God could only get His Church out of Jerusalem into Samaria through persecution in Jerusalem. Only so could the protective walls that Churches have ever sought to build up around themselves be broken down. Will it indeed take twenty-five years to educate our fellow-Christians into the truth that to become members of the New Israel they must be incorporated into a people elected to serve, save, and suffer?

Lesson 3: THE CHURCH DOES NOT EXIST FOR TRADITIONAL MEETINGS

It is not laid up in heaven that we must have a Guild or Christian Endeavour on Tuesday night, a Women's Meeting on Wednesday afternoon, and a Choir Practice on Friday night. Indeed, it is not laid up in heaven that we must have these meetings at all. Yet we have sometimes acted in Methodism and, no doubt, in other denominations as well, as though the purpose of the Church was to promote these traditional meetings. We have gauged the success of a local church by its number of well-attended meetings, as though this provided the sole criterion for assessing faithfulness to its missionary task. When it has been suggested that the purpose of the Church is not primarily the promoting of meetings but the discharging of a joint mission in the neighbourhood, it has been thought sufficient answer to point to the Women's Meeting, the Youth Club, and the Sunday School as a proof of adequate missionary endeavour.

What I am here maintaining is that the Church exists for mission, and that therefore every activity in the Church has to be periodically examined. Do these meetings represent the best that we can do to train one another for our joint mission and to exercise it? Would not, for instance, those excellent

29

Women's Meetings – those at any rate that are composed solely of regular churchgoers – would they not be even better employed on a Wednesday afternoon, or whenever they meet, in helping the bedridden, lonely, harassed people who live in the Church's neighbourhood, instead of conducting a pale replica of the Sunday service, the members passively listening yet again to a speaker?

Of course Christians need to meet together, supremely in Sunday worship and Holy Communion. But even the use the local church makes of Sunday needs to be periodically examined in the interest of its all-important mission. Instead of two or three, would not one service be more appropriate, that all the members of the Christian family could meet together, and not be split into two or three sections having no dealings with one another? One united service would have the advantage, among others, of enabling the preacher to brief the whole Church for the coming week, embodying in his sermon help for the house group study. Where house groups do not exist – or even where they do – it might be advantageous after this one united act of worship to repair to the church hall. Here the congregation might divide into groups, discuss for twenty minutes what God was saying through the sermon, not only to individuals, but to the local church as a whole, and find an answer to the question, 'Where do *we* go from here in our mission?' as well as to the question, 'What does this mean for *my* daily life?'

Such suggestions as these may not be applicable to your church, but the principle they reflect must be – that the Church must see that all its activities subserve the main end of mission as effectively as possible.

Lesson 4: THE CHURCH'S STRATEGY HAS TO CHANGE

Just as wars are fought in different ways in the twentieth century from those in the tenth, so with the warfare of the Church. The battlefield has certainly changed for the Church. In the medieval village, for instance, the battle took place largely within the church building. It did so because all the inhabitants came to church. Since the people CAME to church, the Church did not have to GO to them. All that was necessary was that the people should hear Christ's invitation, 'Come unto me'. In the twentieth century we are gradually awaking to the fact that we must, like the men of the first century, listen to Christ's other words, 'GO, therefore, and make disciples'. We are awakening to the fact that the Church must have a 'GO' structure as well as a 'COME' structure, for the very obvious reason that people no longer come, are no longer found on church premises to be afforded there the chance of conversion and sanctification.

This book is concerned to suggest that house groups could well become an essential part of the 'GO' structure of the Church, as they were in the first century. I do not think that we should regret that times have changed. We are being invited, it is true, to a far more exacting kind of churchmanship, but it will prove a far more rewarding one (see Chapter 10). The challenge to this more costly kind of churchmanship is being made to a Church coming of age, though still barely twenty centuries old. We hear frequent references these days to Bonhoeffer's tantalizingly brief allusions to a world come of age. There is by no means agreement as to what precisely he meant, but there is certainly need to hear clear teaching on the subject the Church come of age. Symanowski can use this language in his recent book, referred to above. Professor Leonard Hodgson wrote in a similar vein fifteen years ago in *The Doctrine of the Atonement*. He pointed out that the early Church went out into a world where both Jew and Gentile considered the purpose of religion to be the securing for the devotee of eternal bliss and salvation. The Church gradually succumbed to this interpretation of religion. It came to think that it was fufilling its function by being 'the ark within which believers could sail safely through the stormy waters of this troubled world with a guaranteed safe passage to the heavenly shores.

'So deeply ingrained was this notion of religion in the human

31

mind that nineteen hundred years have not been enough for the Spirit of Christ to eradicate it from our thought. The individual man must grow through self-gaining to self-giving in a single lifetime; it takes longer for states to grow through the assertion of independent national sovereignty to effective membership in a world-wide community of nations. In one lifetime the Christian must learn that being saved he is saved to serve. The Church has needed a longer adolescence to realize its self hood as the fellowship of forgiven sinners. If it now knows itself to be the redeemed community, has it as yet fully grasped the truth that it is redeemed in order that it may give itself to the service of mankind in the name of God?

'For many reasons I am inclined to think that this twentieth century is the stage in the church's history at which God wills us to make the step forward of grasping this truth.'

Professor Hodgson meant that the Church is now on the threshold of maturity, ready to give herself for the world. She is about to come of age, no longer controlled by the self-centredness of childhood. He proceeded to spell this out in more detail by asking some questions of churchgoers.

'Do we in actual fact and practice think of the Church – of our baptism, our confirmation, our Bible reading, our worship, our communions – as all existing in order that through us God may be at work in His world, working for its redemption and perfection? If I were the rector of a parish, instead of a professor in a university, would my congregation and I think of ourselves as bound together to care in God's name for the welfare, both temporal and eternal, of the community in which we were set, not interested in ourselves, but sharing God's interest in the redemption and perfection of His creation? Or would we fall into the temptation to think of the world as existing for the Church instead of the Church for the world, and only be interested in our neighbours in so far as they could be used for building up the life of the Church?'

Professor Hodgson concludes that when 'the priest allows himself to slip into that attitude, or when priest or layman allow themselves to think that the Church has fulfilled its function if it has ministered to the salvation of their own souls, in them the Church is suffering from arrested development.'[1]

Is your local church suffering from this 'arrested development', or is it coming of age – coming of age, that is, not in the sense that it no longer needs divine aid, for it will always need that, but in the sense that it has gained a maturity in which it can be at leisure from itself, set free from the shackles of childhood to promote the welfare of others? In the medieval village the Church was, on the whole, able to enjoy a placid childhood and just say to itself, 'Come and receive'. As a full-grown being it must say to itself, 'Go and give'.

The long quotation from Professor Hodgson's book provided a summary of the main points in this chapter. The questions for meditation and discussion need no further elaboration.

1. HOW FAR CAN WE CARRY THE ANALOGY OF THE CHURCH AS AN ARMY?

2. DO YOU AGREE THAT THE CHURCH EXISTS PRIMARILY FOR THOSE WHO DO NOT BELONG TO IT?

3. HOW LONG IS IT LIKELY TO TAKE TO CONVINCE PEOPLE OF THE TRUTH OF THE FOUR LESSONS PROPOUNDED IN THIS CHAPTER?

[1] *The Doctrine of the Atonement*, Nisbet, pp. 94–95.

4. Regionalized House Groups and their Witness

THE time has come to be more specific, though not dogmatic. In giving an outline sketch of *one* way in which the teaching of the preceding chapters can be put into practice, I am emphatically not wishing to imply that this particular expression of the teaching is the *only* valid expression of it. I am quite aware that the model portrayed in this chapter will not fit some situations, and will have to remain a far-distant objective in others. I offer it because it seems to me the most obvious and the most desirable expression of the Church as fellowship and mission in a large number of districts, and because it happens to typify the kind of house group of which I have had most practical experience. If this particular model is no good for your area, a description of it may at least serve to demonstrate in practical terms the teaching of the previous chapters, perhaps at the same time stimulating you to think of a type of house group more appropriate to your district.

Notice the title of this chapter and of this series. The emphasis is on evangelism, the declaring of the faith. When we hear the phrase, 'preaching the gospel', we think straight away of preaching in church, or on radio and television, some public utterance by an accredited speaker about God and His offer in Christ of salvation. We may also understand the phrase in a further sense, the proclamation of the gospel in the daily lives of individual believers, for Christian living is an indispensable witness to the gospel. To these two well-known aspects of evangelism this book has been proposing the addition of two more, mutual ministry (see Chapter 2) and joint ministry (see Chapter 3). Here, then, are four ways of proclaiming the gospel. We can not afford to dispense with any of them in these days, when the Church is battling against heavy odds. Not only do we need all four, but, as we shall see in Chapter 10, we need the mutual and joint ministries to increase the effectiveness of the public preaching and the individual witness. The purpose of the chapter is to describe the witness of regionalized house groups in terms of mutual and joint ministry.

Something needs to be said at the outset about the word 'regionalized'. By it we mean that each group is composed of those residing in the area in which it operates. The primary reason for this rule (to which there should be no more than a very occasional exception) lies in the nature of the witness of the group. As we shall see, for a group to witness through the mutual ministry of its members, and for a group to discover and try to meet the various existing needs in its neighbourhood, local residence is essential. A firm insistence, therefore, on this principle of regionalization will serve as one way of underlining the fundamentally evangelistic aim of the enterprise.

The group witnessing through mutual ministry

At the end of Chapter 2 we began to explain how the Fourth Gospel represents Jesus as teaching that the world's attention would be drawn towards Him when His disciples loved one another, and were seen to love one another. 'By this all men will know that you are my disciples, if you have love for one another.' That comes from John 13:35, and there is also John 17:22–23: 'The glory which thou hast given me I have given to them, that they may be one even as we are one, I in them and thou in me, that they may become perfectly one, so that the world may know that thou hast sent me and hast loved them even as thou hast loved me.' Such words to Christ's little group are paralleled, we suggested, by St Paul's astonishing words in I Corinthians 12:12, where he appears to be saying that when Christians are interrelated like the members of a human body, functioning harmoniously in love, then we have not just the presence of the Church, but of Christ: 'So it is with Christ.' Make this body Christianity visible, the conclusion would appear to be, and Christ is proclaimed.

Through regionalization this body Christianity can be shown to the world and men pointed to Christ. If there is a caring of the members for one another, not only in the weekly group meeting but outside it as well, it is conceivable that people in the neighbourhood will become aware that this Jesus, who can make His followers so love one another, must have great power. As time goes on the whole neighbourhood may become aware that in its midst there is a community of the friends of Jesus, a community in which the natural divisions of humanity, race, class, sex, and age are transcended, a community in which the demons of loneliness and self-imposed isolation which infest so many urbanites have been exorcized, a community exhibiting a holy worldliness as it marries religion to the home and to service of others.

This impression will not of course be given if Christians indulge in their mutual ministry for sheer self-display, 'in order to be seen by men'. It will only be given if their Christianity is so real that it appears to be the most natural thing in the world for them to love their fellow-believers for Christ's sake. It is such real Christians who are bidden 'Let your light so shine before men, that they may see your good works and give glory to your Father who is in heaven' (see Matthew 5:16 and 6:1).

The most effective group witness to Christ will need not only such devoted Christians but also Christians of different denominations. If full witness to Christ and His power to reconcile is to be made, then the group must consist of members drawn from all the branches of the Church represented in that neighbourhood, as well as of men and women, old and not so old,

rich and not so rich. ('One-class' districts make this last require-
ment difficult.) We cannot limit ourselves, least of all in this
ecumenical age, to purely denominational groups. If in much of
this book I seem to be envisaging only house groups attached
to the local church of one denomination, I do so partly in the
interests of the maximum possible lucidity, partly because it may
very well be that one local church has to pioneer this kind of
experiment. On the other hand, the success of *The People Next
Door*[1] in many districts suggests that often house groups could
be planned from the outset on an interdenominational basis.
Where, however, one church has to go it alone, other Christians,
with the consent of their ministers and local churches, ought
to be brought in as soon as possible. When the enterprise becomes ecumenical it should not prove too difficult to adapt the
kind of advice I propose to give about, for instance, the role
of the minister in house groups, to the more complicated
situation obtaining where ministers of different denominations
are co-operating.

Though the organizing and sustaining of ecumenical house
groups will prove a more complex operation, the advantages of
these mixed groups will easily outweigh the disadvantages. Not
only will the witness be a fuller witness to the unity which Christ
gives His followers, but it will be a witness more easily seen,
since an interdenominational group can obviously be recruited
from a much smaller neighbourhood than a denominational
one, and in a smaller neighbourhood the group has a much
greater chance of becoming known.

Mutual ministry outside the group meeting will show itself
in an increasing variety of ways. When a group member is in
hospital, or ill at home, other members will do everything they
can to help the patient and his family – without overdoing it or
fussing. Again, a young couple attached to the group will not
find themselves short of baby-sitters. Given a group leader who
sets an example by entertaining and visiting his members,
mutual caring will generally look after itself. Many Christians

[1] M. Dunnett, André Deutsch.

37

discover, as they did in the early days of the Methodist class meeting, a quality of fellowship they had not dreamt of and, through this unexpected experience, come to know Christ in a new and deeper way.

Lest any reader who is not by nature gregarious suspects that so much friendship would be quite overpowering, he can be assured that true Christian love is perceptive and not suffocating. I have never come across a case of any sensitive Christian feeling smothered with kindness by belonging to a group, though I have seen many people's personalities begin to blossom in a new experience of imaginative acceptance by their fellow Christians. In practice most people are too busy to drown a fellow member in innumerable acts of kindness. Fellowship has to be qualitative rather than quantitative, not least with a house group bent on service to those who are not members of the group.

Sometimes this qualitative fellowship can be a very costly business, for the members will wish to stand by one another in case of need. One member of a group in Yorkshire, a shop-girl, was required by her employers to falsify prices in a sale, making the reductions seem larger than they really were. She asked the other members of her group what she ought to do. They decided that, as a Christian, she could not help to promote dishonesty, and that if she were dismissed for refusing to falsify the prices they would stand by her, even to the extent of finding her full wages until she obtained another post. They kept their promise when she was dismissed. This inspiring story seems a faithful application of I Corinthians 12:26-27: 'If one member suffers, all suffer together; if one member is honoured, all rejoice together. Now you are the body of Christ and individually members of it.' The details of such an exercise in corporate responsibility may not become known to the neighbourhood, but the presence of such a spirit within the group will soon begin to tell outside it.

The most difficult sphere in which to show forth body Christianity may well prove to be multi-storey blocks of flats, those

38

'vertical receptacles' referred to in the Paul Report (borrowing the term from Bertolt Brecht). Perhaps here Christian witness will have to take the form of a yet more intensive mutual ministry as well as joint ministry, such as was practised by a community of five young Methodists sharing a flat in the Honor Oak Estate in London who went out to work every day like their non-Christian neighbours, but pooled their possessions and sought to be the body of Christ in those 'vertical receptacles'. Here we have what is implicit in the ordinary local house group made fully explicit.

Hendrik Kraemer, in *A Theology of the Laity*, sees little Christian cells as the counter to the lack of community in so many areas. 'Outstanding traits of modern society are loneliness and massification. Both belong together. They imply an irrepressible drift towards virtual or actual nihilism, inner emptiness and loss of real sense of direction.' Many sociologists would echo these words.[1] Kraemer goes on to indicate the nature of the Christian answer to this challenge: 'The direct approach to these deep-seated diseases has no great promise, because the de-religionizating of vast sectors of people in modern society has deep-seated and long-range historical causes.

'The indirect approach by really *being* communities of mutual upbuilding, of witness and service, by building in the desert of modern life genuine Christian cells, is the one indicated. . . . The Church cannot aim at conquering, but must aim at interpenetrating the world and so communicating with it. The way for the institutional Church to get into the stream is, it seems, to confront incessantly the official local congregations, whether in urban, suburban, middle-town or rural environment, with a simple question. What does it involve to be a Christocratic brotherhood? Not a place where religion of a certain brand brings people together at stated times for stated activities, but a brotherhood where everybody finds his or her place, as in I Corinthians 12, and where the creative fact is the living Christ,

[1] See the Paul Report's summary of Durkheim's analysis of the impersonality of modern society and its results (p. 51).

the Redeemer and Reconciler, who wants to reach the world to minister to it through His redeemed. For the world wants to *see* redemption. It is not interested in being talked to about it.'[1]

This sums up the mutual ministry side of house groups quite admirably. It makes clear that a Christian cell or house group is not just another church meeting but a community of Christians, sharing the life of the world with everyone else, sharing in the Christ-given life with one another, and seeking to extend Christ's Lordship in the neighbourhood by trying to let men '*see* redemption'.

Kraemer's words also form an introduction to the second half of this chapter. If you want to pause for breath at this point and have some discussion or meditation, here are two questions that arise out of the preceding pages:

1. DO YOU AGREE THAT A HOUSE GROUP WOULD WIELD A MORE EFFECTIVE WITNESS IF IT WERE AN INTERDENOMINATIONAL ONE? IF SO, WHY?

2. WHAT WOULD BE THE ADVANTAGES, AS WELL AS THE DIS-ADVANTAGES, OF HOUSE GROUPS ON A RIGIDLY REGIONAL BASIS?

The group witnessing through joint ministry

Mutual ministry must go hand in hand with joint ministry, the service of the neighbourhood by the whole group. Christ and His redemption will be seen even more clearly if the group provides Him with a visible body in which He can once again go about doing good. Moreover, the addition of joint to mutual ministry will kill stone dead the accusation that the group is a little pious in-group, its members exclusively concerned with the saving of their own souls. Again, this service of the neighbour-hood will help to lay a real basis for eventual verbal witness to the gospel, a witness which will go for nothing, as Kraemer indicates, if it is not preceded and backed by Christian needs.

[1] *A Theology of the Laity*, Lutterworth Press, pp. 178–80.

George Macleod, in *Only One Way Left*,[1] tells the story of an Oxford scholar and convinced Christian who threw up a brilliant career in the Colonial Service to run a Boys' Club in London. 'Appalled by the complete aimlessness of even his most senior and responsible lads, he embarked on a course of twenty instructions on succeeding Sunday nights. He gave the Christian answer to "Who am I?" over against all the other answers, spoken and unspoken, that mould the conduct of youth in a modern city. Rest assured he knew the answer, spoke in their own language and obeyed all the laws of "communication". Thirty young men embarked on the course. At the end there were only seven. Finally he asked Bill, the ablest of the stickers, "Have I proved my case?" "Yes, sir," said Bill, "you have proved it up to the hilt: *and it doesn't mean a thing*."' Dr Macleod comments, 'The disembodied Word is not enough. Even correctly stated it is not the Word at all.'[2] Here, then, is at least part of the reason for a joint ministry; to provide some kind of body for the Word.

Before we become more detailed, a word about the *manner* in which the house group attempts to serve the neighbourhood. The members will take heed of the late Dick Sheppard's warning about 'dispensing official love'. They are not out to dispense charity and humiliate the recipients thereby. They are out primarily to cultivate friendships, and the essence of friendship is that it is a relationship in which friends both receive and give. Our Lord, with His instinct for friendship, was glad to be put in debt to the Samaritan woman of whom He asked a drink of water. William Temple, commenting on this episode in the fourth chapter of St John's Gospel, has this illuminating passage: 'The way to call anyone into fellowship with us is, not to offer them service, which is liable to arouse the resistance of their pride, but to ask service from them. Of course the request must be prompted by a real need. The Lord was actually tired and thirsty when He said *Give me to drink*, and drew the woman into conversation by asking her for her help. So social workers have

[1] Published by the Iona Community.

[2] Op. cit. pp. 41–2

found that they cannot bridge the gulf digged by education so long as they live in a style different from their neighbours and offer service. But all is changed when they adopt the manner of life familiar in the neighbourhood and share its needs. One has told of the difference for him when he left his well-appointed settlement in Bermondsey, where he needed nothing which his neighbours could supply, and went to live in a workman's flat. The first evening he wanted a hammer to hang pictures, and went to borrow from the people in the flat below. At once the relationship was different. There was something that they could do for him.'[1]

Members of a group which is a local one will be living in the same area as those they wish to help. It should be relatively easy for them to ask the help of their neighbours, and this not a mere stratagem so much as a desire to strike up a genuine friendship in a natural atmosphere where conditions exist for mutual giving and receiving. I well remember how a house group in Durham City found itself quite unselfconsciously soliciting the help of neighbours. The group had discovered at the bottom of its street a hospital ward full of old men hardly ever visited by relatives or friends. The group was not looking for social work, since it had been founded to do Bible study, but it felt called to meet this need, took the old men under its wing, visited them at least once a fortnight, sent them presents on their birthdays, and generally tried to make them feel that they mattered. After a time the group decided to ask the rest of the street whether they would like to join in and help in this venture, and everyone was invited to a coffee morning at one of the houses. Thereby all the inhabitants became aware of this community of Christians in their midst, a community which was not too proud to solicit aid from them. The story illustrates a number of points which we will take up in due course, but the primary point at this stage is 'enlist the help of those whom you would like to help'. This will show that you are not out to humiliate them or kill them with kindness, but to

[1] *Readings in St John's Gospel*, Macmillan, p. 66.

value them as human beings and set them an example in receiving.

This story of the Durham house group illustrates another fact – that joint ministry does not need to be informed by the anxious activism of a bunch of would-be do-gooders. We do not want to force our attentions on people, but rather to gain an increasing reputation for being available when wanted, to be 'the group for others'. The men in the hospital ward were discovered by accident, not by earnest people seeking to do good at all costs.

The story also suggests that there is more need in a neighbourhood than meets the eye. If you are doubtful whether there is much need in your neighbourhood, *Responsibility in the Welfare State?* might cause you to think again. This is a report of a remarkable survey undertaken by an interdenominational team in Birmingham between 1957 and 1960. The area from which the sample was taken was a very mixed one, as the Report describes. 'It comprises an old-established residential neighbourhood, centred around a mediaeval church; other districts developed in the inter-war period, with both municipal and private housing, and beyond these, a large expanse of post-war housing estates, on some of which blocks of multi-storeyed flats have recently been erected.' The scientifically conducted survey revealed that in at least *one home in four* there was need not being met by either the combined social services of the welfare state or by those of the voluntary social service organizations. Sometimes what was needed was a supplementing of what these official organizations could give, sometimes it was what they were not equipped to provide. Here are some of the unmet needs which existed in Southbridge, needs which are probably to be found in most other districts of this land, needs which a missionary-minded Church with house groups could attempt to meet. We meet Christ in the troubles of others and help them for His sake as well as for their own.

(*a*) *Giving new-comers a sense of belonging.* A house group

43

responsible for just a few streets can usually find out about new arrivals and look them up very soon after they come. *Responsibility in the Welfare State?* suggests that the visitor takes with him a sheet of information about the whereabouts of the shops, community centres and so on. The first visit should be followed up with further visits, even if the visitor is not effusively welcomed. This service is particularly necessary on new housing estates where the old-fashioned neighbourliness has not taken root. Where the new-comers are churchgoers they can be invited to a social gathering in the house of one of the group members, then later perhaps invited to a group meeting, and gradually drawn into the full life of the Church. Thus, in an age when people move house so frequently, one of the main sources of loss to the Church could be dammed up.

(*b*) *Looking after elderly people receiving inadequate attention.* So many women now go out to work every day that there are fewer friends and good neighbours to look after the housebound. This means that there are many old people who would welcome help with their shopping and occasionally with heavy bits of gardening or house-decorating. The Birmingham Report tells of District Nurses, rushed off their feet with so many patients to look after, having to use some of their valuable time lighting fires for the infirm. Here, once again, if the group is a local one, the members ought to be able to discover, without too much deliberate probing, whether they have any neighbours in this kind of need.

(*c*) *Relieving over-burdened mothers.* The Birmingham Report suggests that many of these would welcome the offer of someone to look after young children while they went to visit a sick child in hospital. Many, too, would welcome a night out with their husbands occasionally, if a baby-sitter could be found. Those with mentally and physically handicapped children get desperately tired, and would be glad of an hour or two's relief from time to time.

(*d*) *Helping mental patients to re-settle in the community after*

44

discharge from hospital. This may mean visiting the patient before he leaves hospital, if he is not already known, as well as helping him to take up some social contacts when he comes out – something that many ex-patients find very difficult. The group will need to pick a suitably gifted person for this kind of work.

(*e*) *Befriending lonely people.* There are vast numbers of these, probably in more than a quarter of the homes of this land. As the Report puts it: 'Quite often the chief need may be for someone to talk to. The caseworker and psychiatrist understand the therapeutic effects of letting people who are in trouble pour out their story of woe; and in cases where the trouble is less deep-seated, and no other treatment is needed, the kindly neighbour can perform a real service by being willing to listen, and when the tale is told to listen again.' This of course applies not only to lonely people who have some psychological trouble, but to the many who want friendship but simply do not know how to find it.

(*f*) *Fighting for social justice.* The group can help the neighbourhood by organizing representations to the local council or appropriate body for the improving, maybe, of recreational and housing facilities in the neighbourhood, or for the righting of some social abuses, or for the erecting of a Belisha crossing and the better lighting of a street. The Birmingham Report does not mention this form of community service, since it does not fall within its terms of reference. It is interesting, however, that the five young Methodists who went to live in that block of flats at Honor Oak (see page 39), found themselves not only organizing religious services, running a Youth Club on the premises and so on, but also implicated in a Residents' Association to fight a threat of rent increases.

These are only six of many examples that might have been specified. If you do not think that there are any unmet needs in your area or, at any rate, any unmet needs that people will let you meet, perhaps your Church or local Council of Churches could get into touch with welfare officers and voluntary organizations to see whether they know of people wanting help. Though it will do the Council of Churches no harm to be in close touch with the welfare departments, it is doubtful whether a regionalized group would often find it necessary to have recourse to such an expedient unless it were suffering from what I have called an 'anxious activism'.

We indicated earlier on that there is another and all-important form of joint ministry – our giving, when asked, a reason for the hope that is in us (I Peter 3:15). This may be asked for by a visitor to a group meeting or by a neighbour on the receiving end of some practical help from the group. The group will have anticipated some of the questions that such people will ask, and its weekly meetings will have been directed to working out some of the answers. Such an aim will have saved the group discussions from being cursed with discussion for discussion's sake.

When we are asked for this verbal witness to our faith, then the supreme aim of the group enterprise is beginning to be fulfilled. Here is some of the reward for mutual ministry and the other forms of joint ministry. Herein lies the reason for the group doing its social work, not under the banner of excellent voluntary organizations, but under the banner of Christ (though, needless to say, this does not prevent individual members from helping such organizations as well).

For those who want to meditate or discuss, here are two questions arising out of the second half of this chapter.

1. HOW CAN WE DO GOOD WITHOUT BEING 'DO-GOODERS'? TO WHAT EXTENT SHOULD WE SET OUT TO LOOK FOR NEED?

2. WHAT KINDS OF NEED MIGHT A LOCAL GROUP IN YOUR NEIGHBOURHOOD FIND ITSELF CALLED ON TO MEET?

5. Preparing for House Groups 1 : Facing the Objections

How do we prepare for house groups? How are churchgoers to be persuaded to launch out on this frightening enterprise? Obviously one of the first things to do is to listen to their objections and try to answer them. This chapter lists seven of the commonest objections churchgoers are apt to make, and suggests ways of answering them. Some of the answers outlined here have been foreshadowed, as you will see, in the previous chapters.

1. 'We have never had them before'

Any body of people tends to be resistant to change, not least Christians. Suggestion of change in the future seems to imply for them criticism of the past which is dear to them. Wesley found Methodists objecting to the introduction of class meetings, complaining, 'There were no such meetings when I came into the Society first; and why should there be now?' Wesley's reply is still pertinent: 'We are always open to instruction; willing to be wiser every day than we were before, and to change whatever we can change for the better.'

It is simply not good enough for Christians to shelter behind the dubious maxim, 'What was good enough for our fathers is good enough for us.' For one thing, the Church stands pledged

47

to reform itself as fresh light from the Bible requires, and much fresh light has been illuminating us in the past few decades concerning the biblical doctrine of the Church. For another thing, the mission of the Church, as we were contending in Chapter 3, has to be planned today with full appreciation of the radical change in the shape of modern society. If Christians are to be faithful to their Lord's evangelistic commission they must find new ways of evangelism appropriate to the new conditions of the twentieth century. What may have been good enough for our fathers and perhaps, in its time, even nearly good enough for our Lord, is not nearly good enough today for our Lord, and therefore not good enough for us.

It will probably take more than teaching of this kind to influence the minds of some of the less logical, less spiritually mature, and less progressive spirits in a congregation. It may be, as we shall suggest in the next chapter, that we shall have to start with those who have ears to hear what the Spirit appears to be saying to the Churches, and great patience will surely be needed as we attempt to lead people into radically new ways. But as soon as some neighbouring Churches succeed in the house group venture, it will become correspondingly easier for us to convince the others, as we point to the advantages that accrue from such an ambitious enterprise.

2. 'Why not meet on Church premises?'

It is frequently objected, especially by those who have recently been engaged in raising large sums of money for the erection of churches or their repair, that the church building is 'the house of God', and it is there that spiritual exercises of one sort and another should take place.

Here, perhaps, little more is needed by way of the beginning of an answer than the reiteration of much that has already been written in Chapter 2. The first thing to say is that wherever Christians meet, there is the household of God, for there is the Church. The Church is living stones built up into a spiritual house, whether that Church is in the catacombs, in a gravel pit, in someone's house, or in a consecrated church building. To the objectors we might quote from William Cowper's well-known hymn:

> Jesus, where'er thy people meet,
> There they behold Thy mercy seat;
> Where'er they seek Thee Thou art found,
> And every place is hallowed ground.

Having made this first point we can then go on to assert that, though the Church is as much the Church when it meets in a house as in a cathedral, from the point of view of the Church's mission, it is vital that it meets in houses too. It is so important, as we have said more than once, that the neighbourhood should have a chance of seeing a Christian community at work, both in its mutual and joint ministries. To be visible the Church must go into the arena of everyday life.

This entry of the Church into the arena of daily life does more than make the Christian community visible to men. It teaches people that religion is not something locked up in church buildings but something intimately related to daily life. It is a witness to the truth that participation in the Church of Christ is not a contracting out of normal society for an hour or two on Sunday so much as participation in normal society all through the week. Holy worldliness indeed!

One of the most successful numbers of *Laity*, the bulletin of the Department of the Laity in the World Council of Churches, was the quarterly issue for April 1957, entitled 'The Church in the House'. I quote from the first chapter in this issue to illustrate the way religion can be made 'natural' without ceasing to be 'supernatural' when worship takes place in a home. *Laity* tells of a Protestant house church in Italy, not yet able to build a 'church' but apparently thriving nevertheless. The sermon was not a monologue, but interrupted by spontaneous questions.

'The Holy Communion brought together – as it is meant to do – the sacred and the secular, the holy and the common. The bread and wine were the same as we ate and drank at lunch. The communion-table was the home-made table, where the family who lived in the house assembled for every meal. Even the gestures of "breaking the bread" and pouring out the wine were the same familiar gestures you see during the meals in these Italian working-class families. Everything was so familiar and common during that Holy Communion, and yet "it came to pass, when He had sat down with them to meat, He took the bread and blessed it, and brake, and gave to them. And their eyes were opened, and they knew Him . . .'"

The article in *Laity* goes on to tell how these simple Christians, many of them former Communists, were giving their time and money to build a 'church'.

'It was good to see their eager joy and pride in that building-project. And yet, when I saw the foundation of the planned church-building I could not resist a feeling of sadness: Will this spontaneous Christian community soon be another mediocre Protestant congregation, where an unbridgeable gulf separates the "house of God" from the houses of the different families, the sacred from the secular, the holy from the common, faith from work? Will that church-building accelerate the tendency to replace spontaneity by institutionalism and organization? Will the dialogical proclamation degenerate into monological declamation? And will the laity (the members of the people of God), now on Sundays and weekdays a worshipping, ministering and witnessing community, soon become an aloof church-public, which appears only on Sundays to sit and to listen?'

The author of the article warns us not to regard the house church as a temporary expedient, a second best until the big church is built. We should heed that warning, it seems to me, without going to the opposite extreme and despising the big church building. Given the house church we can surely have also the church building for the centralized Sunday worship of all the house churches, as well as for Sunday School work and other activities benefiting from ample premises. It is not a matter of 'either–or' but of 'both–and'. Both house church and large church are entitled to be called 'the house of God', the house church preventing the large congregation from becoming 'another mediocre Protestant congregation', as the *Laity* article puts it, and the large congregation helping to inspire and sustain the house church.

3. *'There is no room in our house for a group to meet'*

This is undoubtedly a forceful objection on many new housing estates, where the one living-room is needed by the other members of the family watching television or school-children grappling with homework. Nevertheless, it ought to be possible to find at least one home where the room is available. A group does not have to go round the homes of all its members, though that may be a desirable arrangement when it is feasible. And there should be no room among Christians for that form of inverted snobbery which shows itself in undue sensitivity about what more wealthy members may think of a poor, shabby home.

One practical thing can be done to ease the load for those who are not so well-off. It should be made a rule that either *no* refreshments are served at a group meeting, or that no more than a cup of tea and a biscuit be provided. Then, if the group visits the homes of all its members, there will be no competition between the hostesses, no attempt to outdo anyone else, no fear of being outdone.

4. *'I would be dead scared'*

The idea of speaking about religion, even in a small group, is to many people a terrifying prospect. We may welcome the honesty that lies behind this objection, and recognize that, for some, participation in a group may prove a costly exercise at first. But, as the next chapter hopes to show, this fear can be largely overcome in practice groups on church premises; in such groups, where no one is obliged to speak, everyone almost invariably does.

5. 'I should hate to be in a regionalized group with Mrs So-and-So'

This is best treated as another honest remark. There are indeed some temperamental incompatibilities that are difficult even for Christians to overcome, and maybe, very occasionally, there will have to be exceptions made to the regionalization rule.

On the other hand, by pointing out to the objector that staying in the same group as Mrs So-and-So will be a way of witnessing to the neighbourhood that Christ is able to break down all middle walls of partition, and that one of the prime points of a group is to witness in this way for Christ, and that to have a good time with congenial companions is not the primary object of the exercise – all this may persuade a mature Christian to stick it out and perhaps overcome the difficulties. We might add that a rigid insistence on local groups does prevent the formation of cliques, even more so if regionalization helps the group to be evangelistic, and evangelism succeeds in bringing a constant stream of fresh blood into the group.

I feel that we have to be firm on this rule, if not quite inflexible. We are playing for very high stakes, and we have to be daring enough to ask the very best of Christians in the interests of the Kingdom of God. They are, after all, being invited to join an army, not a cosy little club. Maybe this firm policy will prove to be a case of the best being the enemy of the good, but a milder policy is more likely to prove a case of the good being the enemy of the best, and I doubt very much if anything less than our Christ-inspired best is going to be effective for the mission of the Church, surrounded as it is on all sides by apathy and the cult of the mediocre.

6. 'We have plenty of meetings already'

How very true! (I can speak here only for Methodist Churches.) We may agree that it is no good adding house groups to the plethora of other meetings that comprise the weekly menu of many Churches. The only excuse for suggesting house groups is that they do not constitute yet another meeting, but rather the whole Church going into action in a new and radical fashion. If this claim can be substantiated, and I have probably said enough on that score, then it means that there will have to be a painful pruning of some of the sectional meetings of the Church. Such pruning need not imply that the meetings to be abandoned are poor and useless; they may be good and have served valuable purposes in the past; the choice, here again, is a choice between the good and the best.

As a minister, with some years of experience in different kinds of Churches, I am under no illusion about the difficulties in the way of this proposal. Such a pruning will prove a distinctly ticklish operation, and may well have to be delayed for some time while the process of re-education is going on. Even after this delay it will still be necessary to have some saints around for the pruning ever to take place.

In Old Elvet Church in Durham City, where the house group experiment proved a great success in the end, the leader of the Wesley Guild (a week-night fellowship meeting, which in its palmy days had been a means of getting members on to their feet and learning to speak, but which of recent years had more and more lapsed into meetings with speakers imported from outside) came to me after the first year of my ministry there and said that perhaps we ought to have a change. But then the late Mr Herring was a saint. He made this offer though the Guild was very much his child, a child which he had nurtured for no less than forty years. I had never suggested to him that the Guild should be buried but God gave him the grace to make this offer which opened the way for something more relevant to the needs of a new age. If that offer had not been made, the start of the group experiment might have been delayed for some years, perhaps indefinitely, until enough people had been taught to think along the lines summarized in the opening chapters of this book.

I have no hesitation in saying that in my opinion sectional

meetings (women's meetings, men's meetings, etc.) are not meant to provide permanent resting-places for their members. They may well have an important place in first drawing people into the circle of the Church, but the time should come when such people are ready to witness for Christ, to advertise the end product of Christianity to the world – the fact that in Christ 'there is neither male nor female; for you are all one in Christ Jesus'.

The Bishop of Woolwich, in a stimulating book written some time before *Honest to God* and called *On Being the Church in the World*, argues in the same vein about sectional meetings: 'Our parishes are for the most part collections of individuals; or, if these are brought together, it is in organizations. These latter are not units of the whole Church in miniature, but sectional groupings founded on some specifically limited basis of sex, age, or interest. No one could possibly call them *Churches*, though they may sometimes try to act like Churches, and we have the theologically dubious practice of corporate Communions for special organizations and societies – as though anything other than a *Church* could celebrate the Eucharist. By contrast, the house Church is essentially of the same mixture as the lump, except that the area of natural community is small (e.g. a street) and may, in these days when communities are often not geographical at all, be outside the parish structure altogether (for instance in an office or factory).

'I believe that the theological recovery of this idea of "the Church in the house" is one of the most important tasks of our generation. Whereas the organization is an optional extra, of the *bene esse* of the parish, I believe that the cellular structure of the Church will be rediscovered as a necessity of its life.'

John Robinson goes on to affirm that the house church is not only an instrument of evangelism but the Church in its very essence: 'We have a defective idea of the house Church if we *define* it as something which is a half-way stage to the parish Church. Rather, it is a vital cell within the Body itself, which should be reflecting in microcosm the *whole* life and activity of the community of the Holy Spirit . . .'[1]

Bishop Robinson, you may feel, is less than just to sectional meetings, but he has, it seems to me, pointed to their great limitation in stressing that they cannot, because of their peculiar membership, represent in anything like its fullness the family life of the Church, where age, race, sex, and rank are transcended. The house group, on the other hand, represents the rich nature of the Christian community in a way that sectional meetings cannot, and therefore it can lay claim to the title, 'The Church in the house'.

The remedy, then, for too many meetings is for Christians to concentrate on the few that are most important, and house groups may be counted among these. If your local church is going to embark in a big way on the time-consuming experiment of house groups, some old-type meetings in the church may well have to be buried. Christians must be left some time for family and civic life. Even the use the local church makes of Sunday must not escape this 'agonizing re-appraisal' of the structure of its life. One united service should be sufficient (though this creates difficulties, I realize, for Junior Church teachers) and the rest of the day Christians can devote to time with their families, or to preparation for the house group study, or to mutual and joint ministry.

7. *'There are too few intellectual people to run house groups'*

The presence of people trained to think clearly and to a conclusion is of course an enormous asset in a group, provided that they are dedicated Christians. But more important still is spiritual maturity, love for the other members, enthusiasm for the Lord's work, real Christian conviction. The whole of a group's life is not Bible study. The house group is to be thought of also as an action group, which is how, perhaps, some groups should start, finding themselves eventually driven back to their

[1] *On Being the Church in the World*, S.C.M. Press, p. 85.

Bibles in order to provide themselves with more adequate answers to the questions their members are asked on their rounds of mercy.

A group, in short, probably wants at least a clear-minded person for a leader, but he or she need not necessarily be highly educated. Some of the leaders of Methodist class meetings were virtually uneducated men, and their masters and employers were sometimes to be found under their leadership. Such leaders received education of another kind in their experience of God, an experience they nourished with a constant reading of the Bible, their hearts stimulating their minds.

The quality of leadership today can be enormously improved by some initial training, as we shall indicate in the next chapter. But in some minute village churches and chapels, as well as in some larger town ones, there may not seem at first to be much suitable material for the leadership of a modern house group. In this eventuality, house groups might be worked on a circuit basis, or a sub-circuit basis, stronger churches making temporary loans of leaders to weaker ones. Anglican-wise, we could talk of similar loaning within a deanery or within a group of parish churches where a group ministry is being practised. Better still, of course, for *all* Christians in a village to unite in house groups. Leaders would probably emerge through this pooling of local Christian resources, with some initial training by the ministers.

Seven Aunt Sallies are enough for one chapter. Group discussion could centre round any of the seven. No. 6 might prove a stimulating opening subject.

6. Preparing for House Groups 2: Ways of Initiating Groups

AFTER some months spent in instructing the local congregation about the Church as a missionary fellowship, and house groups as the prime expression of its corporate mission, the time may come for the minister to attempt to implement his teaching (providing of course that he is convinced that groups are possible in that church). As a wise minister, he may well decide not to plunge his people headlong into house group activity, but seek to initiate them into it gradually. Occasionally it may be true that church members are sufficiently advanced in Christian understanding to go straight into the front line, but even then they may be unwilling to venture forth immediately. One church differs so much from the next that it is difficult to begin to generalize about the way to initiate groups, but here are some examples of ways in which they may begin.

1. The minister taking a Church Fellowship meeting into a home

This expedient has the obvious advantage of accustoming people to religious exercises in a home atmosphere. It helps to remind them that religion and ordinary life should not be strangers to one another. It causes them to recognize that every house can be the house of God, and they can sing Cowper's hymn, 'Jesus, where'er Thy people meet' with a new conviction.

E

This had to be our pattern at Kings Cross Halifax 1961 - 1985.

It may also convince them that religious conversation flourishes better round a fireside than in an uninspiring and perhaps cold church vestry.

I found that this method worked well in a Durham colliery village, where I was the Methodist minister. After a year or so on church premises, some ten of us invited ourselves into the homes of non-churchgoers for an evening. We were always most warmly received by our hosts. It seems to me that if a house group experiment got no further than this it would have accomplished something significant and most worth while. In addition to the benefits mentioned above, contact was made with non-churchgoers, while the churchgoers learnt something of what it means for the Church to go out into everyday life, meeting people at the heart of their existence, in their homes.

Such home meetings can be varied in character. Ours mostly took the form of simple exposition of Scripture followed by discussion, in which our hosts would sometimes join. Ernest Southcott, in his exciting book *The Parish Comes Alive*,[1] relates how meetings in people's homes often centred on the celebration of Holy Communion. Often non-confirmed people were prepared to have these celebrations in their homes, even though they themselves were not allowed to communicate. In Chapter 6 of his book Mr Southcott emphasizes one of the benefits from this exercise which we have already spoken about more than once – the marrying of religion to daily life. 'In the houses in Halton people have said, "I *see* the connection between what goes on in church and what goes on outside now.". . . "I *see* my house as part of God's world now."' People converted to such points of view are well-grounded for the more exacting tasks of mutual and joint ministry, with no trained minister at hand to help.

2. *The regionalizing of existing class meetings*

In many parts of Methodism class meetings are still functioning, sometimes on church premises, sometimes in homes. Once

[1] Mowbray.

the teaching of the Church as a family and an army has been accepted, it may be possible for the minister to reorganize the classes on a local basis and imbue them with a missionary zeal for the neighbourhood in which they meet.

3. Gathering Christians together in every locality

Though a Methodist class leader often does not 'meet his class', nor a parish visitor ever see all his flock together, what harm would there be in suggesting, after the list of people to be visited has been revised on a regional basis, that the leader (or visitor) should invite everyone round to his house for a coffee evening, and then ask those assembled for any suggestions about service for the neighbourhood that they as Christians ought to be undertaking. Perhaps the Methodist leader and his counterpart in other denominations might even arrange this initial meeting together. Such an enterprise would seem to follow naturally from the ecumenical venture of *The People Next Door*.

As we have said previously, to get Christians at this local level engaged in some practical service may be a more effective way of forming groups than inviting them straight away to Bible study or group discussion, which for many of them would be quite a terrifying prospect. What begins as a Christian action group will very likely become also a Bible study group in time, as the questions of non-Christians find the group members wanting in answers. The minister may even be requested to preach more doctrinal sermons.

4. Preparing for two years on church premises

The method that I am now going to outline in considerably more detail is the one of which I have had most experience and which I think may prove the most obvious way of advance for many local churches, certainly for many of those that are fortunate enough to have a number of rooms on their premises.

59

The training that I am about to describe should ideally take place once a week, but it can function on a fortnightly basis, alternating perhaps with more traditional church meetings which people are loath straightway to relinquish altogether.

All those prepared to do some simple Bible study gather together in a large room. They have with them a duplicated sheet of notes on a Bible passage, together with three or four questions for discussion. They have been encouraged to use this sheet in their times of private devotion during the week, and they come to the meeting with at least some of their homework done.

The passages of Scripture chosen for study each week are well known, so that the trembling participants in this strange new enterprise may find a little self-confidence. The Twenty-third Psalm, part of the Lord's Prayer, or part of the rest of the Sermon on the Mount, a famous parable, St Paul's Hymn to Love, or the very important passage on the Church mentioned in the previous chapter (I Corinthians 12), or any other passages with which they may be expected to have at least a superficial familiarity, will fill the bill. The questions for discussion on the passage chosen need to be simple and practical ones, such as will be most likely to get the uninitiated talking.

The meeting begins with a short prayer followed by a two-minute introduction to the questions, so that the people are given a clearer idea of what they are to discuss. The minister can be in charge of this opening part, for the company are going to spend the next forty minutes or so *without* him. They are to disperse to the various rooms available in little groups, preferably of not more than six persons, under previously appointed leaders, and to return after the allotted span prepared to report their answers to the questions.

Newcomers to this exercise will invariably declare that they will never open their mouths. The wise minister does not dispute this statement, tells them that they do not need to speak unless they feel like doing so – and is not surprised to learn later that they have been the first to talk! In our Durham experiment all the thirty-five people taking part spoke in their little groups from the very first night. Some had left school at an early age, few could boast of advanced education.

Part of the secret of this method of exorcizing the dumb spirit is to prime the leader to do as little talking as possible and to elicit comments from his group members wherever he can. *There is not the slightest need for the leader to give an address*, for the members are expected to have done their homework and be ready to tackle the first question, to throw into the pool tentative answers they have already arrived at, as well as the problems that continue to vex them. The most the leader should do is to present the question and explain its meaning, if it is not already crystal clear.

Given wise leaders, and given the absence of the minister, the groups will probably have had sufficient discussion at the end of forty minutes *briefly* to report their findings. (The group's reporter must be warned not to weary other groups with a long résumé of all the processes of thinking in his group.) The minister can then comment on the substance of the reports, indicate where the discussion might have gone deeper, or where the questions have not really been answered, and encourage the groups wherever possible. After handing out sheets for the following study, he can close the meeting with another short prayer. It is not essential to sing a hymn during the proceedings if a deliberate attempt is being made to get away from the associations of an ordinary type of church meeting. It is most important that the meeting should not last too long. If people know that they will be away within the hour they are more likely to come. *Characteristic groups go on long.*

After a few sessions of this kind the participants will have had a taste of Christianity in terms of the body of Christ. They will have experienced something like the mutual ministry portrayed in I Corinthians 12:12–27, knowing now the 'feel' of group discussion. Leaders will have been discovered and afforded experience, experience being the main school for learning to lead. Of course this is only the beginning; not yet the deep fellowship of a localized house group; not yet the experience of fellowship produced by joint service outside the group meeting. Nevertheless the first step has been taken across the threshold into what is for many a quite new world. To their surprise they find that they enjoy the experiment. They even conclude, if our experience in Durham was at all typical, that they prefer group work to the more conventional Church Fellowship meetings. Harder work seems to bring greater rewards. If they have begun to talk about their faith to some purpose, if they are beginning to share with others their insights and their problems, then they have reached a new stage in their spiritual pilgrimage. As we shall be seeing in Chapter 10, an expressed religion means an impressed religion.

Two years of this kind of activity on church premises will not prove an excessive period. There is much to be said for 'hurrying slowly'. Experience is needed in group discussion and Bible study. The foundations of the future enterprise need to be well laid. The dangers of plunging straightway into missionary house groups are considerable, even if the participants appear unusually competent. If a prompt initiation of house groups seems imperative, half a dozen sessions on church premises would appear to be essential, if only to make sure that the participants really know what they are aiming to do. Some laying of foundation stones will prevent jerry-building, some initial training will help to prevent the house group fizzling out after a year or two for want of a thought-out rationale. What is more, meeting together on church premises helps to underline the fact that the house groups are the local church (or churches) going into action at certain points, and not a number of freelance commando units.

At any rate, two years' preparation proved most beneficial in Durham. When the fledglings were persuaded to leave their nests and fly, each house group started with a nucleus of people who had practised mutual ministry with one another and had learnt to care for one another. The immediate result was that the five local house groups soon swelled from thirty-five members to round about a hundred. This increase in membership led to the division of the groups into ten separate cells.

As I have already indicated, this preparatory period could doubtless take the form of joint training with other churches who are prepared to embark on missionary house groups. Such a combined operation will naturally need ministers who can see eye to eye on the objectives to be pursued and the means to be employed. But with God all things are possible.

One last point needs great emphasis. It is by no means essential or necessarily advantageous to start with a large number of recruits. There will not be many churches that can muster as many as thirty-five to launch the scheme. This fact need not daunt us. Our Lord concentrated on the training of twelve men – twelve persons, we might add, of not conspicuous ability. With a whole world to save He spent most of His public ministry, it would seem, in private with this little group. Instead of making a world-wide tour, He confined Himself to Palestine, but even there He did not diffuse His energies widely. In the building of His World Church He hurried slowly. He set out to teach those twelve men to love one another and to pass on the good news of God's love to others; in short, to be both a family and an army. He was determined to lay sure foundations

Once, He crossed over into foreign territory, presumably to get away from the crowds and to go into retreat with His disciples. They hid in a house, only to be given away. A Syro–Phoenician woman appeared, begging Jesus to heal her daughter. How Jesus must have groaned in spirit at this interruption, this disruption of His plans for privacy. He hesitated in the doing of good, He hesitated to play the Good Samaritan. Yes, *Jesus* hesitated. The reason is perhaps not far to seek. He had laid down a strict strategy for Himself in the attaining of His objectives. This strategy is reflected in the reason He gave the disciples for His hesitation: 'I was sent only to the lost sheep of the house of Israel.' He might have added, 'And primarily to twelve of them.' By this He did not mean that the Church was to be built only of Jewish bricks, but that the *foundations* of it were. Given

63

Jewish foundations, the gospel must then be preached to all nations. Compare Matthew 15:24 with Matthew 28:19.

The Syro–Phoenician woman threatened to get in the way of our Lord's primary task of foundation-laying. She presented Him with the choice, it seemed, between doing the good and doing the best, between healing her daughter and building a World Church. He simply could not afford to get involved at that juncture in a mission to the Syro–Phoenicians. He could help them more in the long run by not helping them then. If the foundations of His Church were not laid well enough because of too many distractions, or through too much diffusion of effort, then everyone, and not only Syro–Pheonicians, would ultimately stand to lose.

In the end He made an exception to His rule and did the woman's bidding. He may have concluded that the game was up anyway, that He would have to retire from Syro–Phoenicia whether He healed the girl or not, so why not give in to that woman's almost irresistible faith? But the story as a whole seems to reflect Christ's strategy of concentrating on the twelve. As Mark 9:30–31 explains it: 'They went on from there and passed through Galilee. And He would not have any one know it; for He was teaching His disciples . . .'

We are therefore not to be disheartened if only a few initially respond to the challenge to start on this venture of house group training. We may indeed receive encouragement from a most unlikely source, from Fidel Castro! After he had accomplished his successful revolution in Cuba, he reflected on it in this way: 'I began my revolution with eighty-two men. If I had to do it again I would do it with ten or fifteen men and absolute faith. It does not matter how small you are providing you have faith and a plan of action.'

Jesus certainly had faith and a plan of action. So He chose twelve men only, for He was interested in the quality of His foundation stones rather than in the quantity of them. This was His method of preparing for Pentecost – concentrated training reflecting a gigantic faith and a definite plan of action. We should not perhaps expect a revival of the Christian religion today without some kind of comparable preparation. The Holy Spirit will light the fire, but He often needs the fire to be laid.

This chapter suggests at least two questions for meditation and discussion:

1. WHICH OF THE FOUR WAYS OF INITIATING HOUSE GROUPS WOULD SEEM THE BEST ONE FOR YOUR CHURCH? OR HAVE YOU ANOTHER AND BETTER WAY TO SUGGEST?

2. SHOULD YOUR LOCAL CHURCH, IN THE INTERESTS OF SPIRITUAL ADVANCE, ADOPT A FIVE YEAR PLAN OR SOME OTHER WELL-DEFINED STRATEGY FOR ATTAINING SPECIFIC OBJECTIVES?

7. The Role of the Minister

WE have seen in the last chapter the enormous importance of the minister in the various stages preparatory to house groups. He it is who must teach, or remind, his people about the nature of the Church as a missionary fellowship. He it is who must insert into their minds from time to time the idea of house groups as perhaps the best expression of this function of the Church. He it is who needs to get the lay leaders' visiting lists compiled on a regional basis, and he it is who can seek to initiate and control the preparatory Bible study and group discussion on church premises, should that be the most appropriate way forward for his particular church.

It is therefore quite obvious that if he is to play his role in the house group enterprise he must be absolutely convinced that this operation is worth while for his church. If he lacks conviction and enthusiasm he stands little chance of turning the local church inside out, which is what the creation of house groups means. He is an instigator of revolution, and must have his objectives clear and his strategy worked out as far as possible.

Not only this, he will also have to be a good visitor if he is going to persuade his people to march forward with him. It is only when they have come to know him as a true friend in their homes, as someone who is prepared to learn from them, to be ministered unto as well as to minister, that they will find themselves willing to follow him into the unknown. The pastoral side of the ministry is basic to preaching, it is basic to practically everything a minister does, and it is certainly basic to the setting up and sustaining of house groups. Finding people at home and not caught up by television is not as easy as it was, but many ministers find it possible still to be excellent visitors.

This chapter attempts to describe in some detail the minister's role *after* house groups have been created. One of the first things he must do is to compose a Bible study outline, or an outline on certain aspects of Christian belief and practice, assuming that his groups are not exclusively engaged on social service of one kind or another. There are quite a few such outlines and other study material available from the Churches' publishing houses, but the great advantage of the minister composing his own is that he can tailor it to the particular needs of his people (providing, of course, that his pastoral work has given him an intimate knowledge of them). As we saw when we were describing the preparatory sessions on church premises, with these group discussion outlines it is best to concentrate on the more familiar parts of the Bible, if Bible study it is to be. If the course is on Christian belief, the Apostles' Creed lends itself very easily to several weeks' study and, like the Sermon on the Mount or I Corinthians 13, has the advantage of being known, if only superficially, by the group members. As with Bible study, each week's page will provide some simple notes, bringing out only the main points in the interpretation of the particular clause in the Creed, and concluding with some questions which the notes will help to answer.[1]

Having supplied all the members of the house groups with an outline, the minister can then supplement the study with his Sunday sermons. If the groups are studying the following week, 'I believe in God the Father', the sermon can be devoted to aspects of the doctrine of God's Fatherhood. The preacher will

[1] See Appendices B and C at the end of this book for a specimen study outline and for examples of study material available from the publishing houses.

67

find that house group members will listen intently, not least the leaders. Not only will the sermon give a boost to the group discussions, but those discussions will in their turn cause his sermon to be remembered. As the saying goes: 'There is no impression without expression.'

The sermon will not only be referred to in the subsequent group discussion, but it will be summarized for the benefit of members not able to be present at the service. If the preaching is so arranged that the sermon follows on the groups' discussions, then perhaps it will be listened to even more eagerly, the the ground being so well prepared; on the other hand, it might have been of more value to the group discussion if it had preceded it. Where, as in Methodism, a minister cannot always count on being in his pulpit every week, arrangements can sometimes be made for the other preachers to preach on the appropriate subject.

In addition to the weekly preaching, the minister may find it possible to take many of his group members to a retreat before the beginning of the autumn session. In Durham we used to travel up to a guest-house in Weardale and spend a day apart from all the usual distractions in order to have a preview of the material we were hoping to tackle in the following months. The value of the expedition was immense, enabling us to see the work of our local church in a detached setting as well as priming us with information.

It may be possible for the minister to have briefing meetings with his leaders once a week, when he can prepare them for the next piece of group study. We never seemed to find time for this in Durham, but it is obviously most useful when it can be fitted in. What is quite imperative is that the minister should keep in the closest touch with all his leaders. He can telephone them the day after their group has met, find out how the meeting went, who was present, who was absent. He can talk over difficulties with the leader or arrange to do so by appointment. He can find out what the group leader would like to do. 'Could he look up So-and-so who is ill?' 'Could he go and encourage So-and-so whose enthusiasm seems to be flagging?' 'Could he visit So-and-so who has expressed a desire to join the group?'

The minister may agree to go to the next meeting of the group to try to give some help with the intellectual difficulties or other problems of mutual and joint ministry. These visits to the groups should be rare, for a reason to be mentioned later. If possible they should be limited to one a quarter. When the minister does visit the group he can use the opportunity to impress upon the members that theirs is a missionary task, that the group exists not primarily for them but for those who do not belong to it. This is a desperately difficult lesson to learn and constant re-iteration will prove necessary.

The minister's advice will obviously be called for when the group's regular membership passes a certain number. The ideal number for a group is probably between six and eight. After it has passed eight it tends to become a public meeting and there is less opportunity and less incentive for some of its members to contribute to the discussion and decision-making. What is more, in many homes eight people in the living-room is nearing the maximum possible intake, and the urge to add to the number, which will activate a missionary-minded group, is correspond-ingly diminished. In short, the time comes when it is necessary for a Christian cell to bisect. Such division is a most painful business, from which any group which has experienced deep Christian fellowship will shrink. But if the minister has succeeded in the difficult task of keeping the missionary aspect of the group's ministry well to the fore, it will manage to divide itself, preferably on a regional basis. The two halves can then proceed to grow, and the injection of new blood into them will have this advantage among others, that there will be no danger of cliques forming, a constant danger with a group of static membership.

The minister's advice will be needed in planning the local strategy of the group. Is, for instance, the group going to try to grow by bringing in church members of all kinds, or is it going to restrict its membership to only those convinced Christians who can adapt themselves readily to group activity? Which method is the more likely to attract the non-Christian into the group? This is a most difficult and tricky question and demands all the wisdom that the group can call upon.

The minister's role is thus quite crucial in both the creation and sustaining of house groups. The fact that he is setting in motion a process of decentralization and devolution does not detract from the importance of his role. On the contrary, he is leading his regiment, even though largely from behind, with motives infinitely superior to those of the Duke of Plaza-Toro! He is continually pushing his troops up into the front line of ministry. His pattern of ministry faithfully reflects the teaching of Ephesians 4:11–12: 'And these were His gifts: some to be apostles, some prophets, some evangelists, some pastors and teachers, to equip God's people for work in His service, to the building up of the body of Christ' (*N.E.B.*). That is to say, there are some special ministers, like apostles and prophets, whose function it is to get the rest of the members of the body of Christ ministering. These special ministers might be called 'minister-producing-ministers'. The growth of the body can be measured in proportion to the success today of the special or ordained ministry in getting all the members of God's laity to minister: 'Bonded and knit together by every constituent joint, the whole frame grows *through the due activity of each part*, and builds itself up in love' (Ephesians 4:16; *N.E.B.*).

The ordained minister gets the other members of the body of Christ to minister in the ways I have indicated by placing them in little groups under wise leaders who say little and elicit much. He further evokes ministry by staying away from the group meetings, breaking this rule only on rare occasions. He stays away from the group discussion in the preparatory stage on church premises, and he stays away altogether when house groups are formed. The reason is plain. If the minister is there, everyone will expect him to do the talking. After all, he is the expert, or supposed to be. Even if they do not expect him to do the talking he almost certainly will! If he stays away, then there is a far greater incentive to all the members to speak and minister to one another. Only by keeping away can the minister begin to turn the sheep into shepherds, the inarticulate into articulate Christians.

Perhaps the truth of all this is reflected in those surprising words attributed to our Lord in St John 16:7: 'It is to your advantage that I go away, for if I do not go away, the Counsellor will not come to you.' We find it hard to understand how it could be to anyone's advantage that Jesus should go away from them. How often we wish that we had been with Him in the flesh! How advantageous that would have been for us! What our Lord is saying may amount to something like this: 'As long as I am with you, you will rely too much on me. You will let me do all the talking and witnessing, whereas you yourselves are now ready to witness after all the teaching I have given you. If I go away from you, you will have to stand up on your hind legs, become shepherds instead of sheep. And when you prepare to witness for me you will, through the Holy Spirit, come to dwell in Me and I in you much more intimately than when you were just near me physically.' If this is the right meaning of Christ's words, if it was expedient for the disciples that He went away from them, it is no doubt also expedient that the minister should keep away from his people much of the time. By so doing he can coax them into ministry. And when he has done that, a new stage in their spiritual experience has been attained, which in its turn means an enrichment of their ministering. On this theme, once again see Chapter 10.

In these days when the active role that the New Testament requires of the laity has been rediscovered, some Christians wonder whether there is any place left for the specially trained and ordained minister. Perhaps this chapter has succeeded in showing how crucial a role the minister has to play in the renewal of the Church. Though the departure of the pastors from the German Evangelical Church in Silesia (see page 18) may have had an immediate and beneficial effect in forcing the laity into ministry of many kinds – ministry into which the pastors

71

should have coaxed them long before – the important question really is, 'How long was this lay ministry effectively maintained without the help of trained ministers?' Or to put the question in a slightly different way, 'What should have been the role of the pastors when and if they returned to their churches?' Their role, as I conceive it, should have been that of trained trainers; should have been to sustain the churches in their ministerial activity and to improve its quality; above all should have been to give the local churches a fundamental missionary structure by means of house groups or some other appropriate evangelistic agency.

Without trained trainers I cannot see a radical renewal of the church lasting for long. The more we raise the status of the laity in the interests of renewal, the more, not less, we are going to need trained ministers – yes, and full-time ministers too. Those who talk of part-time ministers for this age obviously are not seeing the renewal of the Church in terms of the type of evangelistic outreach outlined in this book.

What we need, then, is far more ministers who are able to delegate responsibility, who refuse to be in the centre of every church gathering, who know how to lead from behind. We need men prepared to concentrate all their energies on the local church, that as its spiritual temperature rises the rest of the community may begin to feel the glow. Their evangelism will be bonfire evangelism! To get a bonfire going, as every gardener knows, it is necessary to gather dry material for the nucleus. When this is alight damper material can be piled on it which will burn because of the hot nucleus. The minister, like our Lord, will probably succeed in doing more for the world by concentrating on training a small nucleus of Christians than by getting himself involved in numerous other excellent pieces of service, Syro-Phoenician healings and the like.

One final thing about this conception of the minister's essential role. It will necessitate a longer stay in one church than four or five years, unless the house group enterprise is being run by a team of ministers. Continuity is essential in this work.

It would be tragic if a minister who had worked up a house-group enterprise by himself was succeeded by one who failed to see eye to eye with this conception of the ordained ministry and the renewal of the Church, who failed to sustain the missionary enthusiasm of the groups by visiting their members, planning the Bible study, preaching on its main themes, working in close accord with the group leaders and so on. Some groups might survive for a time, but front-line work is exacting work for those not used to it, and the temptation would be for many group members to relapse into the second best and revert to meetings with imported speakers on church premises. Such a tragedy would have a moral – showing how indispensable the right kind of minister is to the proper renewal of the Church.

The discussion for this week will obviously revolve around the question of what an ordained minister really is and does, or should be and should do. Here are suggested questions on this theme:

1. HOW ESSENTIAL IS THE ORDAINED MINISTER TO THE CHURCH AS IT IS USUALLY RUN TODAY?

2. HOW ESSENTIAL IS THE ORDAINED MINISTER TO THE CHURCH WHICH IS BEING RENEWED THROUGH HOUSE GROUPS?

3. WHAT QUALITIES DOES A MINISTER NEED TO BE A GOOD LEADER? WHAT HAS HE TO LEARN FROM OUR LORD AND HIS STRATEGIC PLANNING? (The group may care to refresh its memory of the last section of Chapter 6.)

8. The Role of the House Group Leader

WHAT does it take to be a leader? The answer might appear fairly simple, but the social psychologists have not found it possible so far to agree upon any particular list of the requisite qualities. One expert can describe leadership in terms of 'intelligence and good judgement, insight and imagination, ability to accept responsibility, a sense of humour, a well-balanced personality, and a sense of justice'. Another expert picks on such qualities as 'power to co-ordinate, power to express the common aim, impartiality, power to delegate, power to reflect the progress of the group'.

Not only do the various lists of the social psychologists fail to coincide, but not all of them correspond to historical reality. There have been outstanding leaders who were singularly deficient in a sense of humour, and who certainly did not have well-balanced personalities! Well may Cartwright and Zander conclude, 'On the whole the attempt to discover the traits that distinguish leaders from non-leaders has been disappointing.'[1]

J. A. C. Brown believes that 'it is meaningless to talk of "leadership" as if it were a psychological trait, something within

---

[1] *Group Dynamics*, Tavistock. For more on this subject from the social psychologists see, for instance, Josephine Klein's *Working with Groups*, Hutchinson University Library, 12s. 6d., and J. A. C. Browne's *The Social Psychology of Industry*, Pelican, 4s.

the individual, which some people have and others do not or have in only a negligible degree. The word makes sense only when we specify to what end and in what circumstances the leader will be expected to act.'[1] We will follow this line in the present chapter.

Our leader is in charge of a group of Christians pledged to communicate the gospel through mutual and joint ministry. The qualities he will need are to be determined in the light of the nature of this particular enterprise. Obviously he must be a Christian. Quite clearly he will need to possess some intelligence and, even more important, a genuine love for people. Sometimes he would benefit from learning about the various insights of social psychologists into the nature of 'group dynamics'. He must have the support of the minister and the local church. Last, but by no means least, he needs to have grasped the nature and purpose of a house group together with his precise role in the attaining of the group's objectives.

We will take up these various points in turn.

1. The group leader needs to be a Christian

He or she should be a believer, and thus a practising member of the body of Christ (see Chapter 2). As a committed Christian he may still have doubts and difficulties about the Christian faith, and perhaps it is as well that he can sympathize with the many people who encounter stumbling-blocks in the way of assured Christian belief. Nevertheless, he is one who can say, 'I believe; help Thou my unbelief.' He will be aware that he is a sinner in need of God's mercy and he will know something, if only a little, of the reality of divine forgiveness and the power of Christ to 'break the power of cancelled sin'.

2. The group leader needs at least a modicum of intelligence

He may not be an intellectual, or an expert in Bible knowledge on Christian doctrine, but he should be capable of absorbing some knowledge, given proper help. He certainly needs to

[1] See Chapter 8 of this book.

be able to think clearly in order to direct group discussion and to take the lead in planning the group's outreach into the neighbourhood.

3. *The group leader needs to have a large heart*

This is even more important than having a keen mind. He must be someone with a gift for friendship, someone who is prepared to receive from others as well as to give to them, like Jesus with the Samaritan woman and Zacchaeus. He needs to be someone who will bring the best out of the group members, make them *all* feel that they are accepted and valued for what they are. He will set an example of caring for other members of the group, calling upon them in their homes, visiting those who are sick, entertaining and receiving hospitality. Such a leader will be loved. Being loved and trusted he will be able to persuade his fellow-members to do difficult and costly work for Christ.

4. *The group leader should have had a course in group dynamics*

So say many people who are knowledgeable about this branch of social psychology. I do not regard this training as absolutely essential, if only because there are any number of excellent leaders who have never heard of group dynamics. If they were to hear about the findings of this modern science some of these excellent leaders might be tempted to remark that social psychologists spend much of their time in elaborating the obvious. But what is obvious to a born leader may be of help to someone else who has to acquire the techniques of leadership the hard way, and even the born leader may be glad to have his intuition and instinct backed up by the laborious researches of the psychologists. It is true that the best training for someone not born to lead is to see a good leader at work and to practise leading under his direction, but the group psychologists have still a part to play, as long as they do not make their pupils so self-conscious about techniques as to cause them to forget that group activity is a highly personal exercise.

76

It is useful to analyse the various possible roles that participants in group discussion can perform. There is room for the *expert* in Bible knowledge or Christian doctrine who can, where necessary, amplify the notes on the Bible passage or the Christian doctrine. Then there is the *facilitator*, the person who probes the expert in order to elicit further information or clarification for the sake of the weaker brethren in the group; or who 'facilitates' the discussion in other ways, such as asking people for their opinions about the practicability of a section of Christ's ethical teaching. The *co-ordinator* comes into action towards the end of a discussion, bringing together the various views that have been expressed and the facts upon which they were based, the summary being designed to lead to some conclusions and decisions. We may also include the *heart-warmer*, the person who exudes *bonhomie* and perhaps some light relief, who makes everyone glad to be present and is, generally speaking, most useful for group morale, even though he is sometimes incapable of seeing the point in the discussion, or keeping to it even if he does see it. Happy the group that possesses different members for all these roles. (See the next chapter for an imaginary reconstruction of such a group discussion.)

Under the title of 'group dynamics' the minister may include, for the purpose of leadership instruction, all that helps to make a group 'tick'. Not only point 4, but points 1 to 3 are also very much part of this modern study; so are 5 to 7.

5. The group leader should be appointed by the minister and the local church

This is important, partly to ensure that the house group enterprise is kept well within the orbit of the local church, and partly to strengthen the position of the leader should this be necessary. In practice leaders are not difficult to select since there are generally so few suitable candidates available. Because no one is particularly anxious to volunteer for this exacting work, there is not likely to be any jealousy engendered by anyone's appointment. Provided that the leader is a likeable person, he will be gladly accepted.

6. *The group leader must have grasped the purpose of the house group*

This we have described in previous chapters as evangelism through mutual and joint ministry. Another reason for the local church appointing the leader through the minister is that a group might very well choose an unsuitable leader who has no understanding of the purpose of the group. The leader must be one who fully realizes that the group does not exist primarily for the individual edification of its members, and that at all costs it must be prevented from lapsing into a cosy little clique. He must constantly exhort his fellow-members to put their evangelistic task first, insisting that only as they do so can they be truly edified, only as they do so can they become a true fellowship, only as they do so can they fulfil their mission to the neighbourhood.

7. *The group leader must understand his precise role in the attaining of the group's objective*

As the role of the ordained minister is to lead his regiment from behind, so it is the role of the group leader to lead his platoon from behind. The good group leader is essentially someone with an instinct for delegation, for pushing others into the front line, for activating the passive, and for inspiring confidence in the timid. Of course he is very much with the rest of the group in the fight, but his purpose is to get everyone fighting.

Sometimes, indeed, it is necessary for him to lead his platoon from the front – when, for instance, he sets an example of caring for the members of the group, or takes a lead in the group's service of the neighbourhood. He is the natural person to serve as liaison officer between the group and the minister, whom he asks to visit prospective recruits or deserters, or to visit the group itself on occasion, as we explained in the last chapter. The leader must also do his best to maintain a weekly meeting of the group throughout most of the year. In this endeavour he may not have to take the initiative, for as soon as he has managed to get the group going on joint ministry its members will see that they must operate for more than the winter months, and that they will need to meet at least once a week to report on the progress of their neighbourhood service and to plan further work. Apart from this they will probably come to realize for themselves that group study and discussion loses its momentum if it takes place only once a month or even once a fortnight.

It is from behind his platoon, however, that the leader will do most of his leading. He will push others into ministry, and this not from motives of cowardice or laziness. In the interests of promoting ministry he will ask a member to introduce one of the questions set for the following week's discussion. He won't press his request, but after some weeks there will probably be one or two in the group who will be willing to accede to such an invitation. Or he will ask one of the members to lead the group's prayers the following week. He will make the request sound less frightening by assuring such a person that he may read some prayers he has previously composed, or use the hymn-book or a book of prayers. Someone not ready to introduce a discussion question or to lead the prayers might be commissioned to carry out a piece of service for the group in the neighbourhood, visiting a lonely person, baby-sitting, cooking a meal for an elderly couple, or going to see someone in hospital. In such ways the mutual and joint ministering of the group will be fostered.

There are other ways as well in which the leader can seek to activate the members. The creation of a relaxed and happy atmosphere in the meeting will encourage total participation in the discussion. By using all his arts of persuasion to make every member do his homework for the weekly group study, the leader can help to ensure that the whole group comes primed with questions and contributions. In addition, he will sometimes try to bring a silent member into the discussion by asking for

79

his or her opinion on a question. Everyone's contribution he will treat with the greatest respect, even though some of the offerings may be rather feeble and wide of the mark. With the better contributions he will seek to stay by asking the group such questions as: 'And how do we see this working out in practice?' or, 'And what would the non-Christian say to that?' If after all these devices there is still a silent member, perhaps he will be ready to contribute when the discussion gets down to some planning for practical service in the neighbourhood.

In all this the leader seeks to do as little talking as possible and refuses to attempt to impose his views on the group. He is all the time encouraging the members to think for themselves, and though he may have occasion to state his views in a provocative way, he will not seek to pontificate or to hold the floor for a moment longer than is absolutely necessary. His role is radically different from that of a speaker at an ordinary church meeting. If, indeed, he has experience in preaching, he may find it extremely difficult to adapt himself from the monologue technique to the technique of inducing dialogue between others.

His eventual success or failure is to be measured by the number of his words in proportion to the number of the words spoken by the rest of the group. When the group is new the leader may have to do much more talking than when it is experienced. But as time goes on, one or two members may find themselves adopting the various roles of heart-warmer and facilitator, if not those of expert and co-ordinator. Ideally, then, a group leader needs to be able to play all these roles when a group is inexperienced, and to play them less and less as the group becomes more experienced. In the end he is to become the conductor of an orchestra instead of a one-man band, seeking to draw music out of others rather than playing it himself, persuading the players in the first place to leave the auditorium and come on to the platform to make music themselves instead of listening to his solo performance.

The questions arising out of this chapter obviously centre on group leaders. Here are three suggestions:

THE ROLE OF THE HOUSE GROUP LEADER

1. WHAT WOULD YOU CONSIDER THE MOST VALUABLE QUALITY IN A GROUP LEADER – APART FROM HIS BEING A CHRISTIAN BELIEVER?

2. WHAT TRAINING SHOULD GROUP LEADERS BE GIVEN?

3. TO WHAT EXTENT SHOULD THE LEADER'S PURPOSE BE TO WORK FOR HIS OWN ELIMINATION?

9. A House Group at its Weekly Meeting

THE group is meeting this evening at the home of the leader and his wife, Mr and Mrs A., who own a small grocery shop. There are nine in the group, but Mrs H. will not be coming as she is in hospital. Her husband, a gardener, is present. Then there are Miss B., a typist, and her boy-friend, Mr I., who is a bank clerk. Mrs F. is present, the wife of a solicitor who considers himself an atheist and will not come to the group. Mr M. is in the Civil Service and a confirmed bachelor – not at all an easy person to get on with. Miss E. is a schoolteacher and quite the best brain in the group.

1. General conversation

General conversation takes place until all the members have arrived. The initial period of social talk is of great value, keeping the members of the group in touch with one another and their various activities, but it should not be much prolonged after the time appointed for starting the meeting proper.

2. Opening prayers

On some occasions these may not be appropriate – if there are non-Christian visitors present who might be embarrassed,

for instance, or if the group has just been formed and the uninitiated are dreading the possibility of a hot-house class meeting
or some kind of spiritual beat-up. It is so very important that
everyone should be relaxed and able to be themselves. Prayers
might come naturally at the end of the meeting when they would
not be in place at the beginning, but the leader must be prepared
to dispense with them altogether on some evenings.

On this evening Miss B. is leading the prayers. She is only
twenty, and has never prayed 'in public' before. She was asked
by Mr A. the previous week to perform this service tonight, and
eventually she consented when he told her that she could write
out her prayers beforehand and read them in the meeting, perhaps including the verse of a hymn or a collect. She adopted his
suggestions and gives most of the time (not more than five
minutes, Mr A. suggested) to guided intercession for Mrs H. in
hospital, for various people in the neighbourhood with whom
the group is in touch, for the local ministers, and for other
house groups. The period of prayer concludes with the Lord's
Prayer.

3. Members' reports

The leader asks for these from those commissioned to visit
various people. There are four reports ready. Here are two of
them.

Mr H., the gardener, has been talking to Mr Z., his friend and
neighbour, about coming to a meeting of the group. Mr Z.,
according to Mr H., is hesitant, having heard from his father of
some of the goings-on in the old Methodist class meeting, but
he has promised to think about it, Mr H. assuring him that the
atmosphere is natural and friendly. After this report the group
discusses whether the minister, as well as the group leader,
should be asked to visit Mr Z. and use gentle persuasion. It is
eventually decided, on Mr H.'s advice, to leave Mr Z. to make
up his own mind without further pressure being put upon him.

Mrs F. has been to see a recently widowed woman with three

83

young children who has to go out to work in the evenings to make ends meet. She does not want charity, but would be grateful for some help with baby-sitting. Mrs F. says that the widow is not a churchgoer but would be very glad to have her children taken to Sunday School and might come herself to the monthly family service. The group then discusses how the children are to be conveyed to and from Sunday School and who could help out with the baby-sitting.

This period of reports and discussion may well take twenty to thirty minutes, but important as it is, and important as is the planning for more neighbourhood service of this kind, it must not be forgotten that the group has some Bible study to do and that the formal meeting is scheduled to be over within ninety minutes from its commencement.

4. *Bible study*

The passage set is the well-known Matthew 5:38–48. This starts with Christ's teaching about turning the other cheek and then continues: 'And if any one would sue you and take your coat, let him have your cloak as well; and if any one forces you to go one mile, go with him two miles. Give to him who begs from you, and do not refuse him who would borrow from you.'

The group members have been reading this passage during the week, together with the notes on the passage and three discussion questions provided by the minister. We will stay with the group's discussion of the first question which takes up most of the available time. The question is based on Matthew 5:42 – 'Should a Christian always give money to a beggar and a would-be borrower? Mr I. was asked at the last meeting to introduce this question, and told to speak only for a minute or two since all would have prepared for the discussion. He wisely restricts himself to telling the story of William Law, the great eighteenth-century Anglican, who took Matthew 5:42 as a hard and fast rule, eventually giving away as much as £2,500 a year to people in his neighbourhood. (As Mr I. points out, the group must multiply this sum many times to reach the mid-twentieth century equivalent.) The result was that Law demoralized the population, many of whom found themselves content to live off his bounty. This generosity, Mr I. concludes, was misplaced; it did not amount to a real loving of Law's neighbours, but rather the reverse, despite the excellent intentions of the would-be benefactor. What do the rest of the group think?

Mrs A., the wife of the leader (not a great brain but has her feet well on the ground) roundly asserts that it cannot possibly be right in all circumstances to give or lend money. How can a mother, very hard put to it to provide food and clothing for her large family, give away what little money she has? Apart altogether from the effect on the beggar, this could not be the right thing to do. Charity begins and ends at home in such cases. (This hypothetical case which she cites reminds her of another subject of concern to her and she meanders right off the point. Her husband wisely refrains from stopping her, not only because she would not heed him if he tried to do so, but also because a group can stand a small measure of irrelevance.)

It is Mr M. who eventually brings the group back to the matter in hand. (He has proved in the past something of a problem case, causing the rest of the group much exercise in patience. He generally takes the opposite point of view on principle, even when he has not a leg to stand on. Tonight he is much more reasonable, though he is still opposing the point of view so far expressed.) He objects to 'monkeying around' with the words of Jesus. Christians surely ought to take Him at His word. Playing around with the plain meaning of Scripture in this way could be extended to all the sayings of Jesus, and then where would they be, with every piece of teaching explained away? No, Matthew 5:42 means what it says. We must always give to others when we are asked to do so.

Mr A., the group leader, has so far said nothing, but he has noticed that Miss E., though a Scripture specialist at the Grammar School, has as usual shown no signs of volunteering any information, preferring in her excessive modesty to allow others to do the talking. Mr A. turns to her and asks for her opinion. 'After all,' he says, 'you are the expert.' Miss E. is thus brought to comment on Mr M.'s line of argument. We cannot, she avers, take all the sayings of Jesus as hard and fast rules. If we did so, how then could we obey both Matthew 5:16 and 6:2? The first tells us to let our light shine before men (something that the group is trying to do in its service to the neighbourhood) while the second tells us on no account to do good works in public.

This remark makes everyone sit up, though one or two are by now bewildered. Mrs F., a very sensitive and perceptive person, decides to draw out Miss E. further on this matter. Could she tell the group a bit more about the nature of Christ's teaching?

Miss E. replies that the sayings of Jesus cannot all be taken as hard and fast rules, because of the incompatibility of Matthew 5:16 and 6:2. Another example of apparent incompatibility in the Sermon on the Mount would be Matthew 7:1–5 and 7:6. The first passage warns us against judging others, the second tells us to assess certain people as dogs and swine. But, apart from these incompatibilities, Mrs A. has already indicated that literal obedience to 5:42 would on occasion entail a mother letting her children starve in order to help a stranger. As Mr I. has also pointed out, a literal interpretation of 5:42 led William Law to harm his neighbours.

Mr H. explodes at this juncture. He is a warm-hearted character, a quality that will probably succeed in winning Mr Z. for the group, but his forte is not to be found in discussion, where he rarely sees or keeps to the point. He complains that the group is becoming too intellectual. He always gives tramps money, because his heart tells him to. It is not for Christians to tell such poor creatures how they are to spend the money.

Mr I. breaks in to ask Mr H. for his verdict on the story of William Law. Mr H. ignores the interruption and bulldozes on, citing Matthew 5:40 in the process. He would be quite prepared to give away his jacket as well as his overcoat, if someone claimed (though wrongly) that he had stolen his. The group is making a mountain out of a molehill.

Mr A., the leader, has been having some coaching from the minister, and points out that the male Jew wore only two garments, so that a literal acceptance of Matthew 5:40 would make Jesus an advocate of nudism! Surely Jesus cannot have intended us to take his words with such solemn literalism. This must be one of the occasions when our Lord had 'a twinkle in His eye'.

This startling revelation evokes a comment from the only member who has not spoken in the discussion, Miss B., who led the opening prayers. She wonders whether Jesus is giving us not specific rules of conduct so much as painting pictures of Christian character by suggesting possibilities for action in various situations. Miss E. comes in with strong support for this idea, pointing out that many of the most reputable modern scholars would take just such a line as this. Going the second mile, offering the second cheek, surrendering the second garment, giving away the last penny – these are not inflexible rules, but examples of how the Christian spirit, being what it is, might express itself in certain circumstances. The spotlight is not on the the actions but on the spirit that prompts them, a spirit that might express itself in a variety of other ways.

The leader decides that time enough has been spent on this question, the answer to which can be expanded and clarified in the group's attempt to deal with the next question. However, before he can summarize the various points of view that have been expressed and attempt to draw some conclusions, he has to allow Mr M. another word. He wants to know what guidance he can find in the teaching of Jesus for dealing with a tramp who might call at his house the next evening, if Miss E. and company are right in arguing that these sayings of Jesus are but evocative action pictures of Christian character. Mr A. is always careful, as a good leader should be, to make Mr M. feel that he is a valued member of the group, and when he produces a good question like this he must be given encouragement, even though this means prolonging the conversation. (There is indeed more humility in Mr M.'s question than usual, and a striking absence of the normally excessive use of the first person pronoun.) Mr A. stays with the question by asking the other members of the group if they have any answer for Mr M.

Mrs A. asserts that, provided she had enough money to give away after catering for the basic needs of her family, she would take a searching glance at the colour of the tramp's nose and an unobtrusive sniff at his breath, and then probably offer him a good square meal in return for an hour's digging in her neglected garden – if both nose and breath indicated alcoholic intake of no immoderate proportion.

Miss E. agrees with this down to earth approach, but points out that besides the glance and the sniff we need purity of heart if our common sense is to be sanctified common sense.

Mrs F. once again comes to the rescue and asks Miss E. to explain more thoroughly what she means. Miss E. replies that our innate selfishness and acquisitiveness can so easily persuade us that it is not in the tramp's real interests to be given money. We can so easily deceive ourselves and give way to meanness when we think we are being altruistic.

Mr A. then makes his summary of the various opinions expressed, but Mr M. will have yet another word. He wants to know how exactly we can be kept in a state of pureness of heart, of love for God and neighbour. Mr A. rules that this is another question and will be coming up in a week or two's time (by which time he hopes to have had some more coaching from the minister).

Mr H. also wants another word. He thinks that he begins to see Miss E.'s point of view, but he is obviously far from convinced that it is the right one. No doubt he will always continue to give tramps money irrespective of the colour of their noses or the smell of their breath. Mr H. helps to keep everyone in good humour, even though unanimity has not been attained; he and Mr M. have done much to keep the discussion going and to keep it close to practical realities.

Mr A. reminds the group that the minister is due to preach

on Matthew 5:42 the following Sunday morning, and prophesies that he will have at least eight attentive hearers.

5. Planning the next meeting

Mr A. manages to persuade one or two to be responsible for the prayers and the introducing of the questions. If Mr Z. should turn up, all of them are to be ready to scrap what they have prepared should he want to tell the group about himself and his ideas. The leader reminds the group of Horst Symanowski's teaching which the minister is always citing, that Christian evangelism begins with listening to the questions of non-believers. He then concludes the meeting with a short prayer.

6. Tea and biscuits

This evening, refreshments are served at this point. It may sometimes be advisable to serve them at the beginning of the meeting, if it is thought that they would help to break the ice with visitors. If they are served at the close of the meeting conversation can continue, but no one is obliged to stay on after the cup of tea.

At the end of this chapter we may pick out some features of this imaginary – though, I hope, not untypical, group meeting.

(a) *Everyone joins in the discussion.* This is partly because the group is a small one, with only eight present. It has not yet grown to public meeting size, and it is to be devoutly hoped that it will bisect long before that happens. Notice not only the smallness of the group but also the skill with which Mr A. manages to draw Miss E. into the conversation. It is also pretty plain that the leader has succeeded in getting all the members to do their homework, with the result that the discussion quickly gets into its stride.

(b) *Members help the leader in the performance of the various major roles in group discussion.* Mr A. and Miss E. give information about the Bible passage and the modern theories on it. (Miss E. is obviously the most expert person in the group, and should be able to lead the other half when the group bisects. On the other hand, she must first show that she possesses some of the instinct for leadership exhibited by Mr A. and, to some extent, by Mrs F.)

Mrs F. is distinctly a 'facilitator' of discussion and understanding. She is indeed a most useful member of the group. Mr H. of course plays the role of 'heart-warmer', as to some degree does Mrs A. Mr A. and Miss E. also do a stint of 'co-ordinating', bringing together factual information and the group's opinions on it, in order to help the members to come to some conclusions.

(*c*) *The group membership is very mixed.* Different social backgrounds are represented; so are both sexes and most age-ranges. (Miss B. at twenty is the youngest member present, but there is no reason why younger people should not join when they feel ready to do so.) The group is well constituted to witness to the world that in Christ barriers are overcome, though the presence of a coloured immigrant would reinforce this witness, as would that of Christians who are not Methodists.

(*d*) *The group is seeking to grow.* It can do this because its membership is not yet too large to gather in a typically-sized sitting-room, and also because it has grasped the fact that its role is primarily a missionary one.

(*e*) *The group decides who is to be invited to join.* It has commissioned Mr H. to see if Mr Z. would care to come to the group. The group needs to be prepared for the invited person and to know something about him. It does not necessarily want to recruit all and sundry. This is a very delicate matter, but the truth must be faced that there may be churchgoers who would prove at best to be no more than passengers in an evangelistic enterprise of this kind. If such asked to join the group it would be difficult to refuse them, but that is a different matter from actively courting their membership. The rule for this group is that no member brings along another without first consulting his fellow-members. It is a good rule.

(*f*) *Only biscuits to eat!* This is a strict rule to prevent competition developing as the meeting goes round in turn to the houses of the various members. (If Miss B. and Mr I. eventually marry and have a family, there may be baby-sitting problems which will anchor the group at their home. Even so, though this rules out competition in the provision of refreshments, the rule is better maintained, if only to save the future Mr and Mrs I. excessive expense.)

Meditation and discussion on this chapter could centre on these last six points. Both (*e*) and (*f*) might prove provocative talking points, which would loosen tongues straight away. Or you might like to tackle one or both of these two further questions:

1. CAN YOU SEE A GROUP IN YOUR CHURCH FUNCTIONING LIKE THE ONE DESCRIBED IN THIS CHAPTER? IF NOT, WHY NOT?

2. DO YOU THINK THE LEADER SHOULD HAVE DONE MORE TALKING THAN HE DID? IF SO, WHY?

10. The Renewal of the Local Church through House Groups

'GIVE, and it shall be given to you,' said Jesus. This is His recipe for religious revival and the renewal of His Church. To those who give themselves for His sake and the Gospel's He promised spiritual life and health. It is not without significance that Pentecost came when the disciples had been led to accept Christ's commission to give themselves to the evangelizing of the world.

The foregoing nine chapters have attempted to show in detail one way in which the local church can give itself to evangelism and the preparation for it. This chapter is concerned to show how the local church, when it is so inspired by God to give itself, finds its true self; how when it dies with Christ it rises with Him. We are not going to dilate on the pleasant subject of increased collections and enlarged congregations, though such benefits of mission are by no means to be despised, but to consider six other aspects of the spiritual renewal that comes to a missionary church.

1. The renewal of preaching

In a witnessing church, sermons will be received far more attentively because the hearers will know how necessary it is for them to repair their ignorance of the Christian faith they are now required to explain to others. Such congregational receptiveness, of course, helps the preacher enormously both in preparation and proclamation. Moreover, he knows that his sermons are going to be remembered, not only because of his people's new-found spiritual appetite, but because the substance of the preaching is going to be re-expressed in the weekly groups, especially if the sermon has been based on the group study.

It is true here, as elsewhere, that there is 'no impression without expression'. If we would possess knowledge it must be allowed to pass through us, whether it be funny stories, mathematics, geography, or the substance of the Christian faith. We only really master a subject when we instruct others in it, or expound it in essays and other ways. The reason why so few sermons are remembered is thus plain to see. As a means of education the sermon by itself is ineffective. Admittedly its main purpose is not to instruct so much as to confront men with God in Christ, and this purpose it often gloriously fulfils, especially when the congregation is spiritually receptive. No educationalist, however, would give much for a system which consisted of a twenty-minute lesson per week, for which no homework was done, on which no notes were taken and no essays written, and from which the pupil not infrequently absented himself if he felt like doing something else.

House groups, then, can help to bring preaching back into its own. They can make the congregation far more spiritually receptive and far more educable.

2. The renewal of Bible reading

A witnessing church means a Bible-reading church. Many churchgoers would be honest enough to admit that they see little point in coming to grips with the New Testament, let alone the Old. The ignorance among the rank and file of Christians today is appalling, making preaching that much more difficult for both preacher and congregation. But once put a congregation into a missionary context, once let individuals feel the need to know the Christian faith they have to pass on to others in their house groups and elsewhere, then Bible reading will come into its own once again. No longer will there be need for frequent and largely vain exhortations from the pulpit about reading God's Word. Bible reading will centre around the group study, and each day's readings can form part of the preparation for the weekly meeting.[1]

Daniel Niles used to tell the story of his young son going one day to a fair in Ceylon, where one of the attractions was a wrestling match. After the show the little boy went behind the scenes and saw the Hungarian wrestlers consuming the largest quantity of food he had ever seen men tackle at one sitting. Each wrestler dealt with three chickens as well as other items on the menu. He returned home to tell his father that he would have died if he had had to eat so much. 'Yes,' his father replied, 'you would have died. But then you are not a wrestler.' It is indeed only as we become wrestlers for Christ that we shall gain an appetite large enough to take in serious Bible reading.

3. The renewal of prayer

The Lord's Prayer, it has been said, was given to men on active service. It is when a church has gone on active service for its Lord that not only preaching and Bible study but also prayer come back into proper use. We are told that people tend really to pray only when they are aware of a crisis. The minister can thus help his people to pray by making clear that they live not only in the crisis of personal troubles but in the crisis of the Kingdom of God. They must be helped to understand that they are the front-line combatants. Once again, as with Bible reading, there will be no more need for pulpit exhortations to daily practice.

[1] See Appendix B.

4. *The renewal of religious experience*

This, too, is a by-product of mission, as well as a fruit of re-
vived Bible study and prayer, themselves the by-products of
mission. We explained above how there is 'no impression without expression'. We now need to see that this dictum is true not
only of the knowledge of things, but even more so of the knowledge of God in Christ. We come to know Christ intimately when
we offer Him to others.

Christians so often suppose that they cannot witness for
Christ until they are absolutely sure of Him, until they have this
intimate knowledge. The Bible suggests that this attitude puts
the cart before the horse. We do not become sure of God in
Christ and then witness. Rather we witness for God and *thereby*
become sure of Him. Isaiah 43:10 testifies to this: 'You are my
witnesses,' says the Lord, 'and my servant whom I have chosen,
that you may know and believe me and understand that I am
He.'

John Wesley learned this lesson in 1738 after his return from
his ill-fated mission to Georgia. He began by discovering what
was really wrong with himself. He had been trusting in his own
good works instead of Christ's. Yet he felt that he had no real
faith in Christ. Then, according to his Journal for 4th March
1738, he encountered Peter Bohler, a Moravian missionary, who
further convinced him of his lack of real faith. 'Immediately it
struck my mind, "Leave off preaching. How can you preach to
others, who have not faith yourself?" I asked Bohler whether he
thought I should leave it off or not. He answered, "By no means."
I asked, "But what can I preach?" He said, "Preach faith *till* you
have it; and then, *because* you have it, you *will* preach faith."'
Wesley took Bohler's advice and eventually, on 24th May, faith
in Christ was given to him. His religious experience was to be a
very undulating one, as is that of most Christians, but in the
depths of his being he now knew Christ and could never forget
Him. His happiest and most assured times were when he was
preaching Christ to others.

Bohler, of course, was not telling Wesley to preach what he did not believe, but what he half believed, what he believed, at least from the beginning of 1738, with the top of his mind. He was to preach so that this faith might take possession of the bottom of his heart. Only in witnessing to Christ could Christ take possession of the whole of him.

It is not always observed that Christ's promise to be with men till the end of the world, the concluding words of St Matthew's Gospel, is a promise given to evangelists, men who had obediently accepted His commission to preach the gospel to all nations. Christ comes through the Holy Spirit in a far more intimate way to those who witness to Him in deed and word than to those merely prepared to receive Him, but not to offer Him to others. Christianity is, as George Macleod once remarked, like electricity. We can only possess it if we take off our rubber gloves, stop standing on rubber mats, and let it flow through us. A church intent on mission has thrown away its rubber gloves and mats and so is acquiring a deepened religious experience.

I first became convinced of the truth of all this in 1943 when some seventy of the Methodist undergraduates remaining in Cambridge accepted a challenge to go on campaigns to various churches in other parts of England. The object of the exercise was not to bring people to the front at public meetings, but to establish fellowship groups in the various local churches. We went seeking to foster group discussion and the subject we chose was that of the cross of Christ.

For many weeks each of the eight teams was trained by a Wesley House student in four basic meanings of the cross. From the start it was apparent that many of the undergraduates, though able enough in their academic subjects, had not enlarged their knowledge of the Christian faith since their Sunday School days – a confirmation of the conclusion that sermons by themselves do not educate. But when we began to prepare for mission things happened. Because we were preparing for something that scared us, we began to pray and really to get down to what the

96

New Testament said about the cross. When we eventually went on campaign, though the atmosphere was not an emotional or unnatural one, Christ became a great reality for many of us. Of the seventy, not counting the Wesley House men, some seventeen became ministers and missionaries, and many others became group leaders and lay preachers. We gave, and Christ was given to us. So it can be through house groups.

5. *The renewal of Christian fellowship*

This we can explain in terms of the acceptance of a common Master, a common mission, and a common message.

Fellowship results from the acceptance of a common Master. As we saw in Chapter 2, when through the Holy Spirit we are led to put our faith in Christ, then we are in a position to realize how much we have in common with all others who are Christ's. In this present chapter we have been seeing how the Holy Spirit comes to us with His gifts when we embark upon mission; among His gifts is that of a more intimate knowledge of Christ and a deepened faith. Thus mission is the gateway to a proper faith in Christ, which in its turn is the gateway to a proper fellowship with fellow-believers. The more we know Christ and the more others do too, the deeper will be our fellowship with them; and this deep fellowship in its turn will help to nourish the developing religious experience.

Fellowship will also be strengthened by joint participation in a common mission. As we fight shoulder to shoulder for the faith we shall experience something not altogether dissimilar from the fellowship of the trenches in the First World War.

Fellowship will be further strengthened by the joint acceptance of a common message. As we learn more and more of the Christian faith through group study we shall be further united in a common grasp of the fundamentals of the Christian message.

This intensive fellowship in the house group will spill over into the wider fellowship of the local church. If our group fellowship is the genuine article, and not the false fellowship of an exclusive set, then it will increase the members' capacity for outgoingness in the wider sphere. We shall have more to talk to our fellow churchgoers about than the weather. There will be a sharing of information about the progress of our respective groups and the problems we are up against. Having learnt to care for people in the small group we shall become less inhibited in talking to people in other groups, even in no group at all. The local church will have become a friendly one, in the fullest sense of that word.

6. *The renewal of Christian unity*

If house groups were constituted on an interdenominational basis, the desirability of which we have stressed more than once in this book, the result in terms of the renewal of Christian unity would be enormous. In sharing allegiance to a common Master, in discovering that they had a common mission and message, Christians would be able to put into right perspective the comparatively superficial differences which separate local congregations. Furthermore, meeting in someone's house – on neutral territory, ecclesiastically speaking – would probably prove psychologically more helpful than just visiting one another's churches for the occasional united service, at which the visitors tend to concentrate on all the superficial contrasts to their own church architecture and liturgy.

What is more, such close working together during the week will surely culminate in a demand for joint worship on Sunday, for at least one service. Such weekday unity and fellowship cannot be given a day off on Sunday of all days. House groups constituted on an interdenominational basis will almost certainly pave the way for one Christian church per neighbourhood. Special services will no doubt continue to be arranged for those who require colourful ritual or no ritual at all, but these will be additional to the one common service in which everyone participates. Here the worship can be a blend of liturgical and free prayer, or the type of service can vary week by week.

Perhaps *The People Next Door* experiment will have persuaded some of us that all this is not just a pipe dream. My conviction is that we can see the Church renewed in this sixfold way if we are prepared to fulfil the conditions which the Holy Spirit requires. Renewal will be given to us if we give ourselves to mission. As is often said, the Church exists both *for* and *by* evangelism. It exists by evangelism as fire exists by burning.

Three questions about the renewal of the local church:

1. DO YOU THINK THAT WE CAN HAVE THE RENEWAL OF THE CHURCH AND THE REVIVAL OF CHRISTIANITY AT LESS COST THAN THIS BOOK SUGGESTS?

2. IS THE COST TO OUR LOCAL CHURCHES OF RENEWAL BEYOND OUR CAPACITY, OR MERELY BEYOND OUR DESIRE?

3. WHERE WOULD YOU START, IF YOU WERE THE MINISTER OF YOUR LOCAL CHURCH?

Appendix A. The Traditional Methodist Class Meeting and Where it Needs Modernizing

To append a section on the Methodist class meeting is not to blow a denominational trumpet. If anything, this Appendix is designed to call Methodists to repentance for having abused and then disused this great instrument of Church upbuilding and evangelistic endeavour. It has indeed needed Anglicans of the stamp of Ernest Southcott and the Bishop of Middleton (E. R. Wickham) to tell Methodists of the supreme worth of the class meeting and of its relevance, in modern dress, to the missionary enterprise of today. 'We have learnt,' wrote Mr Southcott in the April 1957 number of *Laity*, 'that John Wesley was right in asking every member of the Church of England to be a Methodical Anglican and attend a class meeting.' The Bishop of Middleton, full of admiration for the missionary structure of Methodism, regards the class meeting as its greatest contribution to the coming great Church. So let Methodists repent! Let some of them learn that to be ecumenical is not to despise and neglect their Methodist inheritance, but to conserve and reform it.

If a trumpet is being blown in this Appendix it is an Anglican one just as much as a Methodist trumpet. After all, it was an Anglican priest called John Wesley who, under God, started Methodism. Furthermore, he was indebted for his belief in intimate forms of fellowship not only to the Moravians, but, among others, in considerable measure to his Anglican forbears. A book that inspired those Anglicans to found the Methodist Holy Club in Oxford was entitled *The Country Parson's Advice to his Parishioners* and written in 1680 by an unknown Anglican priest. Wesley took the following words to heart: 'If good men of the Church will unite together in several parts of the kingdom, disposing themselves into friendly societies, and engaging each other in their respective combinations to be helpful to each other in all good, Christian ways, it will be the most effectual means for restoring our decaying Christianity to its primitive life and vigour and the supporting of our tottering and sinking Church.' (Notice how the Church so often seems to be sinking, but never quite gets to the bottom!)

About the same time as this book came out Religious Societies began to spring up in the Church of England as a result of evangelistic preaching. Among their spiritual exercises was included an opportunity for the discussing of spiritual problems in informal settings. These Societies rose to something like forty in number and influenced the Wesleys considerably when they came to form the Methodist Societies. We may say, then, that though the class meetings were more intimate fellowships than anything in Anglican practice, one of their forbears was certainly Anglican.

This Appendix is concerned to introduce a great many Methodists, as well as Anglicans, to the origins of the class meeting, to assess its virtues and short-comings, and to suggest where it needs reshaping to meet the missionary needs of today. W. L. Watkinson is reported to have said at the beginning of this century in the Methodist Conference, 'The Class-meeting could say to Methodism what Paul said to Philemon, "Thou owest me thine own self."' May the coming great Church be led to say the same thing of such a modernized version of it as we have attempted to outline in this book.

The birth of the class meeting was unforeseen and it took place in poverty. It was born on 15th February 1742, four years after John Wesley's heart was 'strangely warmed' at the meeting of the 'little society' in Aldersgate Street, London. The place of birth was the New Room, Bristol, the headquarters of a Methodist Society. A meeting was being held there to decide how the debt of £150 on the building should be paid off. Captain Foy, one of the sea captains belonging to the Society, proposed that every member should give a penny a week for the quick discharge of the debt on the badly constructed building. Someone objected, as someone generally does on these occasions, that many of the poorer members would find this levy too heavy. Foy then came up with his historic offer: 'True; then put ten or twelve of them to me. Let each of these give what they can weekly, and I will supply what is wanting.' Other members made the same offer, and the whole Society was divided up into 'companies' or 'classes' under these various leaders. It was the responsibility of these 'class leaders' to bring the contributions to the steward of the Society every week after visiting all the members in turn to collect the pennies, or whatever they could afford.

What was begun as a financial expedient soon developed into a means of spiritual oversight. The growing-pains which marked the adolescence of the class meeting were turned to good account. One penny collector found a member quarrelling with his wife and another the worse for drink. (These incidents may serve to remind us that many of the Methodist recruits were pretty raw specimens and were no more than half-converted. Some spiritual awakening had been experienced under the preaching of Wesley or one of his helpers, but it was often in the Society meetings and in the class meetings that complete conversion and commitment took place, if not at the communion services which Wesley came to discover were converting as well as sanctifying ordinances.) These misdemeanours of the Bristol class members were reported by the class leader to Wesley who perceived that the class system could have other uses besides the financial one. As Wesley later reported the incident to his friend, Vincent Perronet, Vicar of Shoreham in Kent, 'It struck me immediately, "This is the thing; the very thing we have wanted so long."' Wesley saw the class system as a means of supervising the growing numbers of Methodists who were becoming far too numerous to be shepherded by himself and his handful of clerical colleagues.

Wesley told Perronet that he called the class leaders together 'and desired that each would make a particular inquiry into the behaviour of those whom he saw weekly. They did so. Many disorderly walkers were detected. Some turned from the evil of their ways. Some were put away from us. Many saw it with fear and rejoiced unto God with reverence.'

This system of pastoral oversight was soon adopted in all other areas where Methodism flourished. Outside Bristol the giving of a penny a week, coupled with a shilling a quarter for those who could afford it, went in the main to charitable and evangelistic purposes.

Another growing-pain of the class system was the difficulty experienced by many leaders in finding their twelve members at home every week. Moreover, in some homes their visits were not appreciated by the non-Methodist members of the household, and there was no opportunity to speak in private with the class member. So it was eventually decided that the twelve members should meet their leader at the same time and place once a week. In this way the class meeting emerged and the system developed.

We may pick out three of the principal features of the class meeting in its prime – pastoral oversight, fellowship, and conversions.

1. Pastoral oversight

In the leader's class paper, or class book, an entry was made weekly in respect of every member. 'A' indicated that the member was absent for reasons unknown, 'B' because of business, 'D' because of distance from home, 'N' because of neglecting to come, while 'P' signified that the member was present. Three consecutive absences without adequate reason involved expulsion from the class and the withdrawal of the quarterly class ticket of membership.

This policy may seem too harsh and authoritarian by today's standards, but some strong discipline was required for the very raw recruits in the Methodist ranks. Here in the weekly class meeting the gains of Methodist preaching were consolidated and increased. George Whitfield, great preacher though he was, reflected sadly on the contrast between the progress of the revival under his leadership and that under Wesley. 'My brother acted wisely. The souls he awakened under his ministry he joined in class. This I neglected, and my people are a rope of sand.'

So convinced did Wesley become that the class meeting was an indispensable complement to the preaching of the gospel – and this may have an important bearing on our devising of missionary strategies for the local church today – that he became loath to preach in those places where no such follow-up appeared possible.

The pastoral oversight of the members consisted not only of the weekly talk with their leader but also of a quarterly examination by Wesley himself or one of his assistants. If the member succeeded in passing, his class ticket would be renewed. It was necessary to show that the member, even though not yet fully converted, nevertheless meant business, that he wanted to be converted, and that he was showing this desire in the way he lived. John Wesley tells us in his Journal for 8th March 1747 how he went about such an examination. 'I visit, for instance, the class in the Close, of which Robert Peacock is leader. I ask, "Does this and this person in your class live in drunkenness or any outward sin? Does he go to church, and use the other means of grace? Does he meet you as often as he has opportunity?"'

Here was a new religious order at work, with Wesley's local assistant meeting the class leaders once a week and learning about the spiritual progress or decline of these travellers towards holiness.

2. *Fellowship*

The early class meetings were stiff and formal. Between the first and final devotions the leader used the hour to talk with the members one by one. Gradually, however, the class became less a court of inquiry and more a family circle. Designed as a financial expedient, discovered to be a means of pastoral oversight, it was destined to be supremely a joyful means of fellowship. So Wesley wrote to Perronet, 'Many now happily experienced that Christian fellowship of which they had not so much as an idea before. They began to "bear one another's burthens", and naturally to "care for each other". As they had a more intimate acquaintance with, so they had a more endeared affection for, each other. And "speaking the truth in love, they grew up into Him in all things, who is the Head, even Christ; from whom the whole body, fitly joined together, and compacted by that which every joint supplied, according to the effectual working in measure of every part, increased unto the edifying of itself in love."' However unattractive we may find certain features of the class meeting, it had the love which covers a multitude of sins. We see by his citation here of Ephesians 4:15–16 that John Wesley knew the New Testament connected its teaching about the Church as the body of Christ with mutual ministering.

3. *Conversions*

As Wesley indicates, the class members did grow up into Christ. What may have been no more than a whetting of the appetite for salvation, given by Methodist preaching, found satisfaction and fulfilment in this fellowship of mutual ministry. In the class meeting people committed themselves to Christ's service, receiving not only conversion but its fruit of increasing sanctification.

In its old age the class meeting exhibited many of the characteristics of decay. Like some very old people it was given to repetitiousness, certain members making the same stereotyped contributions week by week. An acute shortage of good leaders developed in the later nineteenth century when it proved no longer possible to make membership of a class meeting the *sine qua non* of Society membership. Many Methodists, well content to come to Sunday worship and Holy Communion, had no desire to lay bare their souls, not even in an intimate fellowship.

The good things in the class meeting are plain. It practised Christian fellowship of the New Testament pattern, it consolidated the gains of preaching and nurtured the spiritually awakened, it made people articulate about their faith and able witnesses to it in the world. We desperately need it back today – but without its failings, for it stands vulnerable to the accusations of being too inquisitorial, too introspective, and too individualistic.

(*a*) *Too inquisitorial*. Christians today would not stand for a minute examination, especially in front of others, of their conduct and growth in grace. This kind of oversight may not have been inappropriate for the period of eighteenth-century revival with its raw recruits, but this is hardly the modern context. A modern group may well decide of its own accord that a certain amount of mutual discipline, a keeping of one another up to the mark, is a necessary aid to their Christian discipleship, but this is different from having to submit to an official inquisition. Similarly, the members of a group, when they have got to know and love one another, may find themselves voluntarily revealing confidences and spiritual struggles, but this will be different from compulsory confession, and more valuable.

(*b*) *Too introspective*. These inquisitions encouraged an unhealthy subjectivity and introspection. 'My experience', with the emphasis on the 'my', rather than on the Lord who had had dealings with me in the week past, tended to become the vogue. We may think that Wesley's previous practice in Georgia of discussion on a biblical or other religious reading was a healthier exercise than the eliciting of religious experiences that became the fashion after his own heart-warming in 1738. In a period of religious revival a movement can live on testimonies of this kind, but they grow thin and stereotyped when the tide of revival recedes.

By the year 1878 the Methodist Conference came to advocate the use of the Bible in the class meeting; but even then it was patently afraid that the class meeting might become a Bible study circle. That, no doubt, in the opinion of our forbears, would have been a far too objective exercise for the class meeting. But Bible study, or a study of the doctrines of the Christian faith, does at least ensure that we do not get bogged down in the sands of an excessive subjectivity. If properly drawn up by the minister and imaginatively used by the leader, the study outline can be made to connect with the daily lives and experiences of the group members. In the context of the objective study personal experiences can be aired by the members to their hearts' content, and all the better for being spontaneous. In this way a modern group can strike a healthy balance between the objective and the subjective.

(c) *Too individualistic*. This may seem a curious criticism to make of a meeting which practised fellowship in such an intimate way. However, Wesley understood the main purpose of fellowship as the upbuilding of the individual soul in grace. Fellowship for him was primarily a means to individual ends. The individual was saved by means of fellowship, rather than saved into fellowship conceived of as the essence of Christianity and as an end in itself, though both John and Charles do sometimes represent fellowship in this latter way.

The tone of the class reflected that of the Society of which it was a component part. The Society, according to Wesley, was 'a company of men having the form, and seeking the power, of godliness; united in order to pray together, to receive the word of exhortation, and to watch over one another in love, that they may help each other to work out their salvation'. Solitary

107

religion was impossible primarily because individuals need the help of others in attaining individual salvation.

This principle that fellowship is mainly a means to the attainment of the individual ends of the participants was given unmistakable expression in the bands, smaller and more intimate meetings than the classes. In the bands men were segregated from the women, and the married from the unmarried. As though four different kinds of bands were not enough, there was a further, spiritual grading for band members, and membership of the bands, unlike that of the classes, was restricted to the fully converted. This segregation and grading was all devised in the supposed interests of individual sanctification.

It is most important to reflect on this dominant conception of fellowship in Wesley's mind, because it helped to create the ethos which modern Methodism has inherited. This ethos makes it extremely difficult to persuade the members of a modern house group that the meetings do not exist primarily for their own individual edification. (Perhaps Methodists are not the only ones whom it is difficult to disabuse of this idea.) Yet Wesley had far more justification for his emphasis on fellowship as a means to the individual ends of the class members; his situation was very different from ours. *The class meeting did not have to go out and find people; they were sent.* Its task was not to win the outsider but to convert the insider. It had a certain right to exist for those who were its members, for its task was to complete what Methodist preaching had begun.

The modern house group will be lucky if it is sent non-Christians awakened by preaching. Today it has to be the means of the awakening. It has to go right into the arena of everyday life, as did Wesley with his preaching. It must not hide itself on church premises, as has been the habit of some groups; its mutual ministry must become visible and its joint ministry conspicuous, for both are ways of preaching the gospel, of winning men for the fellowship religion which the group tries to exhibit.

Naturally, if a house group is successful in awakening non-

Christians, it will be occupied for a time with its new members; but only for a time, for the newly awakened must be helped to play active roles as quickly as possible in the witnessing group. As we saw in Chapter 10, it is through witnessing that they will truly come to know and believe and understand. The paradox is this, that the group which exists for those who do not belong to it will be the group whose members are most edified. For most of the time, then, put the emphasis on the fellowship's mission rather than on the individual growth in grace of the members. Given the corporate mission, the individual sanctification will look after itself.

As this Appendix is by way of being an optional extra, I have not chosen any questions for discussion. If discussion is required, it can obviously revolve around the question of the main purpose of a group, and in this way sum up much of the thinking that this book may have generated.

Appendix B.   A Short Speciman Study Outline

THIS short specimen outline for group study can provide no more than a rough guide for someone who has not composed a group study outline before, since it is drawn up with no particular local church in mind. It will therefore probably need adapting for local consumption.

This particular outline is designed for the beginning of a house group experiment, and the four passages are chosen with the object of stimulating people to think about the nature of the local church and of house groups as an expression of it. Leaders of groups who use this outline will find background material for it in the first three chapters of this book.

Each week's homework is divided into six parts for those who want to combine their preparation with their daily devotions. This is not an essential feature of a study outline, but it may appeal to certain groups. It has the advantage of making private devotions more purposeful and linking the prayers of each individual with those of the other group members.

'The local church and house groups' could serve as a general title for the four weeks' study. The four weekly titles are as follows: 'The Church of Ministers', 'The Church of Mutual Ministering', 'The Church of Joint Ministering', and 'The Church's Title Deeds'.

The group members should be encouraged to have at least

two modern translations of the New Testament by their side. *The New English Bible* and the *Revised Standard Version* are particularly recommended.

First week's study. Ephesians 4:1–16

THE CHURCH OF MINISTERS

First day: Read over the passage in as many modern translations of the New Testament as you possess.

Second day: Meditate on verses 1–6. St Paul is concerned to explain 'the unity which the Spirit gives' (*New English Bible*). He reminds Christians of the seven cords that bind them together. In verses 1–3 he mentions some ways of expressing this unity. It is, as the remaining verses show, a unity of members ministering in the body of Christ. Verse 1 introduces this theme with the assertion that every Christian has a vocation to be a ministering member. So at this point begin to think about Question 1 for group discussion.

Third day: Concentrate on verse 7 and on the word 'grace'. Notice St Paul's insistence that grace has been given to every Christian, to every member of the body of Christ. (He has given similar teaching in I Corinthians 12:7 and Romans 12:3, which are worth looking up at this point.) Begin to think about Question 2.

Just as every Christian has a vocation to ministry in the body of Christ, so every Christian is also given grace to exercise it.

Fourth day: Meditate on verses 7–12. Grace here may be described as the inspiration that comes to us to serve others, as we behold the love of God shown to us in Christ. Loving Him, we long to serve Him. The more we love someone the more power we have to serve them. Love for someone enlarges our natural capacities. Grace for ministry is this

111

enlargement of our capacities made possible by the love of God.

Fifth day: Concentrate on verses 11–12. While all Christians have a vocation to ministry and grace to perform that ministry, some Christians are leading ministers. The leading ministers in St Paul's time are named in verse 11. Today we should refer to them as the ordained ministry. One of their main tasks is to help all the other members of the body of Christ to fulfil their God-given ministry.

The New English Bible here is almost certainly right in leaving out the comma (not in the Greek original) after 'saints' (the people of God, all members of the body of Christ). It is the saints who are to be equipped for ministry, helped to do the work they feel inspired to do for the Church. You can begin to think about Question 3 now.

Sixth day: Read verses 13–16, concentrating on verse 16. Here we are told about the main purpose of every Christian being given the vocation and grace to minister. This is to enable the body of Christ to grow in love. The body grows 'when each part is working properly' (*Revised Standard Version*), that is, when *every* member is ministering to the whole body. This is the way the body and its members grow up into Christ the Head.

Questions for group discussion

1. What proportion of the members of your local church are passive sheep, and what proportion are really active ministers?
2. Is it credible that every Christian has a vocation and grace for ministry in the body of Christ?
3. If you were an ordained minister, how would you set about trying to equip all the members for ministering?

Second week's study. I Corinthians 12 and 13

THE CHURCH OF MUTUAL MINISTERING

First day: Read I Corinthians 12 and 13 in all available modern translations.

Second day: Read I Corinthians 12:1–11. All Christians are gifted by the Holy Spirit for ministry (verse 7). This was the theme of last week's study. Then we thought of God's grace inspiring men for ministry. The Holy Spirit is the giver of ministry in that He is the bringer of grace. He it is who gives us eyes to see Jesus as the divine Lord (verse 3), to see in Him God's love for us. This enables us, as we saw last week, to love God in return and, loving Him, to wish to minister to others for His sake.

Third day: Read I Corinthians 13, St Paul's Hymn to Love. The basic gift of the Holy Spirit is love. By giving us the ability to love God in Christ He gives us the power to love others for Christ's sake – see I Corinthians 12:26.

Without love none of the other gifts of ministry are any good (13:1–3). Love is the most important gift (verse 13). Love unites the ministering members of the body of Christ. Love is permanent, whereas other gifts will vanish away (13:8–13). Start on Question 3.

Fourth day: Read I Corinthians 12:12–26. Being a Christian, being united to Christ through Spirit-given faith in Him as Lord (12:3), means membership in His body (12:12–13).

Being in His body means both giving and receiving ministry. Thus the Church is the Church of mutual ministry. Being a Christian means that we belong to a fellowship where we are all dependent on one another as are the members of a human body. Everyone is indispensable (12:20–25). Begin on Question 2.

Fifth day: Read I Corinthians 12:8–10 and 12:27–31. Here St Paul lists some of the gifts and ministries which the Holy

113

Spirit evoked in Corinth. They are not necessarily identical to those He evokes elsewhere, where needs inside the Church may be different, though some of them, besides love, will surely be necessary everywhere.

Sixth day: Concentrate on I Corinthians 12:12. Where we have mutual ministry given and received in love, we have Christ in our midst. St Paul does not say, 'So it is with the *Church*' as we might expect him to have done, since he is talking about the Church in terms of a human body in this chapter. No, he writes, 'So it is with *Christ*.'

If Christ is present where mutual ministering is to be found, then showing such ministry to the world is a showing of Christ. This is how St John seems to see it (John 13:35). Think about Question 1.

Questions for group discussion
1. In the light of this week's passage what would you say to a person who claimed to be a Christian without being connected with the Church?
2. To what extent should and could a house group be like the body described in I Corinthians 12:12–27.
3. Do you see more clearly than you did the close connection between I Corinthians 12 and I Corinthians 13?

Third week's study. I Peter 2:1–10

THE CHURCH OF JOINT MINISTERING

First day: Read the passage in modern translations.

Second day: Read verse 5. The Church is composed of living stones, of people, not of bricks and mortar. Begin on the first question for group discussion.

Third day: Read verses 3–8, 10. Verse 4 shows that the Church

114

is composed of people who have 'come to Jesus', the corner-stone. They have come (verse 3) because they have tasted His kindness and responded to it by putting their faith in Him (verse 6). They are thus the people who have received mercy (verse 10).

Fourth day: Read verses 1–2 and 5. The Church is a fellowship. Coming to Jesus the cornerstone means being joined also to the other stones united by faith to Jesus. In other words, Christians cannot have Jesus by Himself. They have to learn to behave in a loving way to their fellow living stones (verses 1–2). They have to learn to minister to one another – see I Peter 4:10.

Fifth day: Read verses 5 and 9. The Church is a missionary fellowship or fellowship mission. It is composed not just of a number of individual priests, but is a corporate priesthood, a 'chosen race', a 'holy nation', 'God's own people' (verse 9). The priests have been joined together as living stones.

All Christians are priests as all Christians are living stones. Priests are essentially go-betweens, introducing God to men. The Church is essentially mission; it exists to 'declare the wonderful deeds of Him who called you out of darkness into His marvellous light'. The 'spiritual sacrifices' offered by the Christian priesthood are not only worship but also evangelism. See verse 5 and Romans 15:16. Start on Question 2.

Sixth day: Read verses 9–10. The Church is the people of God. God has done the choosing of this new Israel, which He has brought into being through Christ. God has given the Church its mission to the world, commanding it, as He commanded the old Israel, to be a light to the nations. Notice how much of the language applied to the old Israel in Exodus 19:5–6 is is here re-applied to the Church. Start on Question 3.

Questions for group discussion

1. How necessary is a Church building if the real Church is made up of living stones joined together?

115

2. Is your local Church geared primarily for mission? Do its members realize that the Church exists primarily for those who do not yet belong to it? What difference would it make if they did realize this and acted upon it?
3. What does this passage tell us about the famous doctrine of the priesthood of all believers?

Fourth week's study. St Mark 3:13–20

THE CHURCH'S TITLE DEEDS

First day: Read the passage in modern translations.

Second day: Read verses 13–14. The Church is *holy*, because it belongs to God in Christ, because Christ calls it into being, because Christ appoints its members to serve Him. It is holy, not because its members live perfect lives – none of them do – but because of its holy Creator and Sustainer. The Church is His show, and is set apart by Him for special work.

Third day: Read verses 16–19. The Church is *catholic* for this reason, among others: that it is made up of so many different types of people. It is meant for all sorts and conditions of men. What an odd assortment those first twelve members were. The biggest difference was between Simon the Zealot (member of the underground resistance movement fighting the Romans) and Matthew the tax-gatherer (the quisling who collaborated with the Roman oppressor). For the unity of the Church in the midst of so much variety see also Ephesians 2:13–16, Galatians 3:28 and I Corinthians 12:13. Though so different, the twelve were taught by Jesus to love one another, and they gradually became a fellowship. Being with Jesus meant that they had to be right with one another. Start on Question 2 here.

Fourth day: Concentrate on verse 14. The Church is *apostolic*,

116

which means that its members are 'sent out' to witness to their Lord in word and deed. They are not only to be with Him and one another in fellowship, but they are also to comprise a missionary fellowship.

One way of being a missionary fellowship is simply to be a visible fellowship – see John 13:35. Another way is to go out preaching in pairs and doing good deeds. Think about Question 1 here.

Fifth day: Go back to verses 13–14. The Church is *one,* as well as holy, catholic, apostolic. It is one because it is Christ's show, His new creation, His bride. It is one because all its members share in His choice of them and His love for them. It is one because it is to witness to men that Christ is the bringer of peace and the demolisher of all middle walls of partition, one because it has a common message.

Sixth day: See verse 20. 'He entered a house' (*New English Bible*). The Church started as a house group! See also Romans 16:3–22, I Corinthians 16:9, Colossians 4:15, Philemon 2, Acts 2:46 and 12:12. Think about Question 3 here.

Questions for group discussion

1. What could a house group accomplish in your neighbour-hood besides casting out the demons of loneliness?
2. Would it be desirable, since the Church is catholic, to include Christians of other denominations in your house group?
3. Do you feel the need of more Bible study in order to be equipped to witness to non-Christians?

Appendix C.   Further Suggestions for Group Study

Books useful for House Groups. (Your clergyman or minister will help in further suggestions and recommendations, and should be able to supply background books and works of reference, and give guidance over difficult passages of Scripture.)

Bible
Some groups have found the Pelican Gospel Commentaries most stimulating – J. C. Fenton, *Saint Matthew*; D. E. Nineham, *Saint Mark*; G. B. Caird, *Saint Luke*; John Marsh, *Saint John*. Others would feel that these are too '"A" Level', and prefer the studies of William Barclay (St Andrew's Press), or the *Layman's Commentaries* (S.C.M.), and *The Manuals of Fellowship* (Epworth Press) issued over the years until 1968 which are intended for group discussion.

General
Faith, Work and Worship (R.E.P.).

Doctrine
David Jenkins, *Guide to the Debate about God* (Lutterworth); Michael J. Skinner, *This is Christianity* (Epworth); H. M. Waddams, *Basic Questions of Life and Death* (Epworth).

Worship
A. R. Couratin and H. de Candole, *Reshaping the Liturgy* (Church Information Office); Douglas Harrison, *The Book of Common Prayer* (S.P.C.K.); Gordon S. Wakefield, *Our Different Ways of Worship* (Epworth).

Prayer
J. Neville Ward, *The Use of Praying* (Epworth); Gordon S. Wakefield, *The Life of the Spirit: A Report of the British Council of Churches Working Party* (Epworth).

The Church
John M. Waterhouse (ed.), *Beware the Church* (Epworth); Colin W. Williams, *Where in the World?* and *What in the World?* (Epworth).

Ecumenism
The *Star* Books, edited by the Bishop of Bristol and Rupert E. Davies (Mowbray and Epworth).

Comparative Religion
Lesslie Newbigin, *A Faith for this One World* (Epworth).

Ethics
J. A. T. Robinson, *Christian Morals Today* (S.C.M.).

119